HAND TO HAND

Hand to Hand

The Longest-Practicing
Reiki Master Tells His
Story

John Harvey Gray and

Lourdes Gray

With Steven McFadden
And Elisabeth Clark

4666-GRAY

To order additional copies of this book, contact:
Xlibris Corporation
1-888-795-4274
www.Xlibris.com
Orders@Xlibris.com

DEDICATION

Mrs. Hawayo Takata

Acknowledgements

I want to acknowledge Rev. Beth Gray for her gentle guidance into the metaphysical world. Mrs. Hawayo Takata showed me that Reiki works, and carefully passed on to me the tradition recovered by Mikao Usui. Richard Moss, M.D. and Brugh Joy, M.D. led me into an appreciation of the outer limits of the physical body, the human aura, and helped me to find the chakras. Rachel Claire outlined the essentials of emotionality in the chakras. Bob Monroe taught me about synchronization of the right and left brain hemispheres. I honor them all for their magnificent contributions to healing and the understanding of healing. I honor and respect my children Kathelin and John for their remarkable ability to grow to adulthood. And I especially want to acknowledge and thank my wife, Lourdes Gray for her everlasting love, and her faith in this project.

John Harvey Gray

My voyage into healing was accelerated by my mother, Adriana Cervantes with her own compassionate actions to-

4666-GRAY

ward the ailing and needy. I acknowledge Beth Gray for her friendship, teaching, and guidance. I acknowledge and respect the friendship of my son Joseph Cervantes, who helped me to grow into a real mother. I honor Steven McFadden for his insights into Spirit, and his vast contributions to this book. I acknowledge Cynthia Popp-Hager for her valuable aid in reviewing and correcting the anatomy sections. I acknowledge Elisabeth Clark for her friendship, and contributions to my own literary clarity. I honor and thank Jayne Ronsicki, Lic Ac., M. Ac., for reading and commenting upon parts of the manuscript. I honor and thank also Cecile Betit of Vermont for her substantial contribution to this book, taping the content of our classes and transcribing the tapes. I honor and thank Brian Bauer for his technical assistance putting this project together. And I want to cherish and honor my husband John Harvey Gray for his faith in my spiritual development, and for his abiding love.

Lourdes Gray

Contents

Introduction

The heart of this book is a healing system called Reiki, a Japanese word that is pronounced "ray-key." While it is relatively new in the West, Reiki arises from an ancient healing art, a system for the laying-on of hands. The principal methods for transmitting Reiki are believed to be hundreds, perhaps thousands of years old, yet entirely necessary and appropriate to the 21st Century. The technique and methods of Reiki were long forgotten until the early 20th century. Through the efforts of Mikao Usui, Reiki was recovered and developed in Japan, so that other people could be easily trained to heal by touch. By now, at the start of the 21st century, Reiki is one of the most rapidly growing forms of complementary health care.

Reiki means universal life force, the energy that is all around us, and within us. Reiki is a gentle, non-invasive, hands-on energy transfer technique which made its appearance in the continental United States around 1973. With properly performed Reiki, energy flows through the arms and hands of the practitioner and into the cells of the person being treated to boost well-being and recovery. Reiki differs from other healing methods in that a special formula is used by the Reiki instructor to prepare trainees for the flow of healing energy, and to protect the healer against taking on the conditions of the person being treated. Reiki is something that everyone can learn. It requires no special prior knowledge, or special ability. It is entirely natural, and well within the range of human capability. The system is so simple and natural that a child, properly instructed, can do it as effectively as an adult can.

A Reiki energy session vitalizes the body's cells. By the end of a single laying-on of hands treatment—which takes about an hour—all of the recipient's body systems (blood, nerves, organs and so forth) are re-charged and operating in a stronger, more normal, more balanced way.

In the 1980s, when John first began to think about writing this book, his inclination was to focus specifically on emotions and the Chakra energy system of the human body. He had been inspired by his involvement with Reiki and seminars with Dr. Richard Moss, the author of a book entitled *The I That is We*, and somewhat later with Dr. Brugh Joy, the author of *Joy's Way* and *Avalanche*. Over the 20-plus years of this book's gestation, however, things changed to the point that we wanted, instead, to share a broad range of understandings related to health and healing. In particular, we want to pass on as comprehensively as possible what we have come to know over many years of practicing and teaching Reiki.

Since the introduction of Reiki to the West in the 1970s, it has proven itself to be an effective healing art. Dozens of schools, hospitals, hospices, nursing homes, clinical settings, and churches, in the U.S. and around the world, offer Reiki. Many educational institutions, including professional nursing associations, offer continuing education credits (CEUs). They have all found, as we have, that Reiki can in many cases eliminate a health problem altogether, and that it reliably speeds the healing process and brings comfort, thereby fulfilling one of the central spiritual injunctions of the Western tradition: heal the sick, comfort the afflicted.

While Reiki can be considered a spiritual technique, it is not a religious one. By that we mean that there is no ideology or dogma associated with the technique of Reiki as it is practiced in the West. A Reiki practitioner can be a Christian, a Hindu, a Moslem, a Buddhist, or any other faith, or even agnostic or atheist. Personal religious orientation matters not at all. Once a person is properly attuned, Reiki energy flows. It can flow along in respectful silence, or amidst the brain wave patterns formed as a practitioner silently prays in the faith of his or her heart. For most people the acceptance of Reiki, we have found, comes not from faith or theory but directly from their experience giving or receiving, and from their observation of its results.

When the healing art of Reiki was recovered by Mikao Usui in the early 20th century, it was called Leiki, for the Japanese language makes no use of the "R" sound. Somehow, somewhere along the way from Japan to the West, the name of the art changed to the word that is now widely known, Reiki. The term Reiki is composed of two words Rei, meaning Universal Life and Ki, meaning energy.

There has been a direct and specific line of development of Reiki techniques and teachings—hand to hand—from Mikao Usui to Chujiro Hayashi to Hawayo Takata. We feel blessed to be direct beneficiaries—from their hands to our hands—of their sacrifices, teachings, and insights. Now it is our honor and pleasure to pass on information about this system to readers through this book. The actual technique of Reiki, however, can only be passed on directly to a student by a qualified and properly trained Reiki instructor. Reiki must be taught in person, and passed on hand to hand.

At the outset, this book documents John's evolution from a nervous, angry businessman to a serene, fulfilled teacher of a healing system, and Lourdes' development as a Reiki teacher and partner. The book also recounts the history of Reiki and its lineage of teachers, and it presents two theorems. The first theorem explores what emotional set-points are, how they are created by experiences in early life, and how they tend to manifest themselves through the course of a person's life. This material expands information about emotions originally identified by Wilhelm Reich, a psychiatrist and spiritual researcher. He found that muscles hold emotions from past experiences, and can cause a person to be stuck emotionally with feelings of grief, anger, jealousy, fear, and so forth. This reality, as we have affirmed through years of work and observation, is a matter of crucial consequence. Held emotions crimp the healthy flow of energy and lead to illness.

The second theorem is a new and logical view of the human energy system, a system known about and worked with for thousands of years in the Orient, and lately confirmed by Western science. In this book, based in particular on John's work, we consider the function and purpose of this energy system, and its relationship with Wilhelm Reich's system of emotionality. We also discuss how the human energy system can be examined to provide important information about the root causes of an illness—a key to healing. It is generally futile to treat symptoms only. As the late Reiki Master Hawayo Takata often said: "Reiki is cause and effect. The practitioner finds and treats the cause; then the effects, or symptoms, are gone."

A foundational premise of this work is our understanding that there is a field of energy around every living thing that is complex and rich in purpose and information, perhaps richer even than the magnificent complexity of the human brain. Why is this a fairly new concept for the West? Perhaps because in the West the practice of healing and the understanding of the body have been based on a Newtonian model of reality. The extrapolation from this model is that the body is a material, biological machine. In this understanding, neither human consciousness nor concepts of divinity necessarily play a role. But that model is incomplete, and Western science is beginning to grasp a wider view.

At the start of the 20th Century with his famous formula ($E=MC^2$) Albert Einstein demonstrated that matter and energy are interchangeable. One may ask, is our reality composed of matter (particles) or of energy (forces of varying frequencies)? What we see now, at the start of the 21st Century, is a cosmic paradox: it's both.

At the time Einstein published his work, scientists strained to grasp the implications of the equation $E=MC^2$. The quest continues among scientists and the public at large. Modern scientists have continued to develop glimpses into the nature of reality through the theories of Relativity, Quantum Mechanics, Uncertainty, and Superstrings. These theories advance the understanding that matter and energy are interchangeable and, ultimately, woven into a single unified field. As the November 1986 edition of Discover magazine put it:

"These theories (Superstrings in particular) have turned the universe into an entity in which all matter and energy, all forces, all people, planets, stars, cats, dogs, quasars, atoms, automobiles, and everything else are the result of the actions and interactions of these infinitesimal linked strings."

In this science-based understanding, much as in metaphysical conceptions of reality, everything is connected, and everything is in dynamic flux. The universe is "a single, unbroken wholeness in flowing movement," as described by physicist David Bohm in his book, *Wholeness and the Implicate Order*. Researchers say this universal connection occurs at the submicroscopic level of the Planck scale, wherein the scale of measurement is to the atom as the atom is in scale to

4666-GRAY

the solar system. What happens to any one part of the vast field of matter and energy which is our reality affects all other parts.

Our personal connection with each other and with all things in the universe is thus not a nostalgic or romantic notion, but is as accurate a worldview as modern physics and mathematics can ascertain at the end of the 20th Century. This worldview—anciently indigenous to mystics by way of insight and contemplation, including the Reiki Masters of old, and now joined by the leading edge of Western science—is so far grasped by only a few people. While the theories are widely known, their implications are generally not taken into consideration in matters of economy, philosophy, health or healing. Over time more people may come to appreciate this emerging sensibility about the nature of our reality. If so, they may naturally employ it as a foundation for decisions and actions.

Without getting deeply into the technical or theoretical aspects of this emerging worldview in our book, we assert that this basic perception changes everything. It is plain that our human lives are composed of both matter and energy. Healing is possible, thus, through both physical and energetic modalities. It is just now, though, that a spark of recognition for this reality is glimmering in the West. Reiki can be a centering point in the midst of this awakening process, because it is a distinct, well-defined discipline which continues to build a track record of success.

What this means to a properly trained Reiki healer is that there is an emerging scientific basis for the human energy system, and energy healing. If a person's energy system is traumatized or depleted, this has health consequences. And just as obviously, a skillful practitioner can supply healthy universal life energy (Reiki) to help another person repair and heal their energy field—and body.

It's not our intention in this book to explore in detail the human energy system and related research. The literature on the subject is already voluminous. Readers will, however, find references to it throughout the book and in our list of recommended reading. In particular, we direct readers to the work of James L. Oschman, Ph.D., whose compilations are cited in the list of "Some Relevant Studies" at the back of the book. He reports on fascinating and well-controlled laboratory experiments showing the existence of a measurable and beneficial effect in healing from the laying on of hands. He also presents solid evidence that laying on of hands is not a placebo or the "power of suggestion" at work, but rather something else—what most practitioners of laying-on of hands would say is a natural flow of life energy that comes through them when they relax and apply their particular technique.

Healing by hands, or energy work, is a tradition that spans the globe, stretching back at least 5,000 years, and in various forms it is still widely practiced around the world today. In *Hand to Hand* we have striven to present the context and the procedures of one specific energy healing discipline, a discipline that we know is effective: Reiki.

Over our years of practice, we have found Reiki to be a profoundly helpful healing art. Thus, now at the dawn of a new millennium, it is our great pleasure—at long last—to offer you the gift of Reiki through this book, hand to hand.

Steven McFadden

Chapter 1
John's Road to Healing

When I was an infant, my father had a habit of reaching out and tickling me in the ribs. Whenever he encountered me in the various rooms of the house, whether I was in the crib or on the rug, he would go for me and tickle. He was a good-natured man and loved watching me explode into spasms of laughter. He didn't realize how much his tickling fingers dominated and hurt me.

Eventually, as conditioning would have it, I began to dread his entrance into any room where I happened to be. I was certain his entry would lead to tickling. Very early in life, gently but steadily, I began to fear what the future would bring. That fear lay the foundation for the growth and maturation of an anxious, nervous and angry businessman. Those years, in turn, led to what I experienced as a blessing of great magnitude: my learning, practicing and teaching the healing system of Reiki over many long and happy years from age 57 onward.

My grandfather, John Cameron Gray, left the family farm in Ryegate, Vermont in the mid-1860s to attend Dartmouth College in Hanover, New Hampshire where he attended school during the day and worked nights to earn his way to a degree and a job as a schoolteacher. He steadily advanced to become a superintendent of schools in Burlington, Kansas. It was there that my father, John Harvey Gray Sr., was born.

My grandfather eventually came back east, first to North Adams and then to Chicopee Falls, Massachusetts. When he was of age, my father followed his father's pathway and studied at Dartmouth for a business degree. In 1910, he got a job with an international bank, first in London and then at a bank branch in Manila in the Philippine Islands, deep in the heart of the Pacific Ocean.

There, my father met my mother, Jettie Arnold Taylor. They were married in 1915 and, according to family legend, I was conceived about a year later as a result of a wild Fourth of July party. My birth date is April 10, 1917. I am an Aries.

Since my father was a manager of bank branches and was often transferred, I spent most of my childhood in exotic locales: the Philippines, China and the island of Java, which is now in Indonesia.

Ten years later, we moved back to the United States, settling in Los Angeles and later in San Francisco, where I graduated from Lowell High School. Dad was a stock market bull in 1929 and consequently lost what was for then a considerable sum, $500,000, in the great stock market crash and depression.

Despite the harsh winds of fortune, the family survived well enough to let me go forth in search of an education. I followed the two previous generations of my family to Dartmouth College, by the Connecticut River in New Hampshire. Like my grandfather, I earned my way through with a job. I was a waiter in the student nurses' dining room. This was my first and only exposure to medical and paramedical subjects, albeit in the most casual of ways, until I studied Reiki much later in life.

Like my father, when I was at Dartmouth I majored in

business administration and took my senior year at the Tuck Business School where I learned to enjoy northeast winters. After college, in 1939, I returned to California, starting work with the Bank of America a year later.

At that time, World War II was brewing for the United States. By March of 1941 I was inducted into the Army. After basic training at Fort Knox, Kentucky, I landed in a tank battalion, which, while I was with it, operated without tanks. I became a clerk and typed away while the unit was based first at Fort Ord, California and then March Field in Southern California. While on a weekend pass in San Francisco, I met Beth Hoffman who later became my wife.

December 7th, Pearl Harbor Day, disrupted many lives. We were all immediately on a war footing with no question about what must be done. I volunteered for pilot training in what was then called the Army Air Force. When I left, the Sergeant Major told me he was sorry to see me go because I was the best typist he had.

I reported to Thunderbird Field in Arizona, graduating satisfactorily from primary training. I moved on to basic pilot training at Minter Field in California. That was something else. There were too many dials in the cockpit for me to keep track of. Things were going badly. The final blow came when I lost my way on a short cross-country flight, getting back to base just before dark. I washed out and reverted to a ground position in the Air force. My application for officer training, however, was approved and I was transferred to Miami Beach, Florida. After the first semester I applied for and was accepted for Statistical Officer training. I finished up the training at Harvard Business School in Cambridge, Massachusetts.

Suddenly I was a Second Lieutenant, shopping for uniforms and bars. Sometimes I think back on that time, remembering the sense of superior status I carried within me and how a little status can go to the head and distort a person's sense of balance, which is often alienating to others and a waste of energy.

Eventually I was assigned to a squadron in the 90th Bomb Group, which flew B-24s on missions in New Guinea. I was the guy who reported plane malfunctions and losses to the Statistical Control Unit (SCU) at 5th Air Force. As time went on, I landed a job at the SCU itself. We moved from New Guinea to the island of Leyte in the Philippines, which amazingly enough was quite close to where I had grown up. The move stirred nostalgic memories. My family had lived in Manila and in the town of Cebu on the island of Cebu nearby.

On the next move of the SCU to the island of Mindoro, closer to Manila, which was controlled by the Japanese at that time, I contracted an acute case of infectious hepatitis. I turned yellow and lost about 20 pounds while I was in the hospital. While there, I learned that I had been promoted to the rank of Captain. The fellow in the bed next to me was an enlisted man who seemed to be just as intelligent and important as me. We talked a lot and my feelings of superiority gradually disappeared.

Shortly after I recovered sufficiently and rejoined my unit, Manila fell. We passed through the city on our way to yet another new headquarters at an airfield in Pangasinan Province. I remember vividly the death stench of the more than 200 Japanese soldiers whose bodies were lying in the main plaza of Manila. I remember how one corner of the central post office building was smashed in by shellfire. I had a sense of how Filipinos must have felt, trapped between the warring Americans and Japanese.

Finally the Germans surrendered, ending the war in Europe. With this ease in the strain of the war, I obtained a 21-day pass to the mainland United States. I went straight back to Beth and married her on Thursday, May 24, 1945, just a few days after setting foot at home. Most of the soldiers who were on leave at that time were permitted to remain in the

United States rather than return to the Philippines. The need for our service had diminished. Shortly after, I resumed active duty stateside in Arizona, the atomic bomb was dropped on Nagasaki and Hiroshima. The war was over. I chose to return to civilian life and was discharged with the rank of Captain on November 19,1945. Dismissing the possibility of post-graduate study, I promptly returned to employment with the Bank of America in Menlo Park, California. I was married and, as with so many thousands of other soldiers being discharged at that time, I was starting a family and needed to earn a living.

I was now a teller at the bank and also the General Ledger Bookkeeper. Life was very civilian. I walked to work. I took great pride in my accurate accounts and my lack of cash discrepancies. Then one day I discovered something that disturbed me greatly. My cash was short ten dollars. I was confounded at this discrepancy. I made a complete count of all the cash in my drawer, rather than just the bundles of bills. For several months after that, I found myself short in my cash as often as once or twice a week. In an effort to prevent these differences, I became very slow and careful in my work. I made a complete count of one denomination at the end of each day, not just the bundles of a denomination but a complete count of all the bills in that denomination.

One afternoon, when I complete-counted my ten-dollar bills, I found I was short a ten in one of the bundles. I then made a complete-count of all of my currency and coins. I came up missing the ten-dollar bill plus a one-dollar bill, a silver dollar, a fifty-cent piece, a quarter and a dime, a total of $12.85. It was obvious to me that someone had taken the money from my cash box. I told the branch manger of my difference. He replied that a crew from the bank's Inspection Department was due in a few weeks, so even though my anxiety around the discrepancies was unabated, I let it be. When the inspectors came, they found that the bank's vault was in single, not double custody and that one man, the assistant manager, took out and put away the cash boxes by himself. A review of his checking account revealed small deposits on the days that one or another of the tellers had differences. When they grilled him, he would not confess to the defalcation, but the evidence was strong enough to get him fired. The vault was returned to double custody and I had no further differences. But because of this, I was terribly slow as a teller and my confidence did not return for at least a year. Anxiety over the future, this time as a possibility that I would have cash discrepancies, was playing a large part in my mind and emotions.

In 1948 I accepted a job in the Inspection Department of the Bank of America. At the time, Beth and I were living in Menlo Park, California where our daughter Kathelin was born a year later. We lived there until 1952, when we moved to Woodside, California, which was home to the family for 25 years. Our son John was born two years later.

My first three years in inspections were spent traveling to bank's branches, reviewing bank and employee accounts. I liked my job but the memory of the $12.85 shortage stayed with me. I was always subconsciously looking for the person who stole my cash.

While in the Inspection Department, I was temporarily assigned as a bookkeeper to Stanford Research Institute (SRI). There, I worked on the emerging electronic banking computer being developed for the Bank of America. My first day, I walked into a building without partitions, packed with wires and vacuum tubes. An open space in the center held a huge drum. This drum was a special-purpose computer, which held the balances, checks and deposits of as many as 5,000 accounts in its memory. Next to it was a counter with a hole in which I dropped, one at a time, checks or deposits. A reader under the counter read the amount printed on the item and the amount was recorded in its proper location on the big drum. Every once in awhile, all the lights on the drum would flash and the SRI developers would look at it and say, "Clobbered again!"

I spent several months at SRI, fascinated by the work. But my constant tension and anxiety were taking a toll. In 1951, perhaps inevitably, I had severe abdominal pains, diagnosed as stomach ulcers. The emotional set-point established in my childhood was aggravated by my worry to the point of crisis.

"Emotional set-point" is a term I use to describe the overall emotional tone of a person. This tone is based on emotional responses to events in infancy and childhood. These responses create an attitude that affects daily life as an adult. My emotional set-point from early experiences was anxiety around getting tickled, which translated itself into anxiety around all future events, including, quite intensely, the missing $12.85.

Western medicine often deals with symptoms, trying to ease them one way or another without looking for the cause. The emotional set-point of a person can often serve as a window, giving us a clear view of root causes of illnesses. In my case, the missing funds situation triggered an emotional set-point that was further aggravated by the tension I felt at SRI. If the same situation happened to someone with a different background, it might not have bothered them as much or at all. But because of my past experience, it bothered me greatly and I got sick as a result.

After a year of diet restriction, I followed the advice of my physician. I elected an operation for a sub-total gastric resection, in which 80% of my stomach was removed. Recovery from the operation took two long months. I then returned to branch work for the bank.

There had been significant benefits to this set of circumstances. The ulcers manifested themselves as they had at various times earlier in my life when I had no control over a painful situation. However, in the case of the cash shortfalls, I had chosen to look for the solution to an uncontrollable situation by complete-counting one denomination each afternoon. Now that was an intuitive act, without a basis in logic. I just felt I needed to do it and I did. My intuitive act paid off. I had no logical basis for engaging in the tedium of that counting, but it turned out to be just the thing. Normally we would count only the bundles of bills, not the bills in the bundles. But from the counting I got a big clue to what was going on, and thus took control of the painful situation by an action that was beyond logic.

After a short time in the branches, I was assigned to the San Carlos branch as Operations Officer. The assignment was close to home at last, and I commuted by car the 10 miles from my home in Woodside. My duties consisted of seeing that the branch operated smoothly. I resolved problems with the customers, arranged training for new employees and searched for the answers to out-of-balance situations. I brought home for overnight and weekend work sheets of listings of checks and deposits, looking for totals that didn't balance. It was a tedious assignment and I was not particularly good at it. One day I was offered a job in the Bank's Systems and Equipment Research Department in San Francisco. I became proficient at computer systems development and programming, and eventually was hired away from Bank of America by Stanford Research Institute at Menlo Park, California.

I left Bank of America in January 1965 having been there for 24 years and seven months. At Stanford Research Institute (SRI), from 1965 to 1974, I did system programming and systems development. I traveled doing projects for SRI and spent several months in Sweden, almost a year in Germany and a couple of months each in Japan and Saudi Arabia.

The course of my life has covered the globe in a variety of different and intensely rich circumstances. Presently I teach and practice Reiki full time, and also write from my present home by Lake Monomonac in Rindge, New Hampshire, with my second wife, Lourdes. I have been teaching and practicing Reiki longer than any other living Reiki Master. The beginning of my education in Reiki took place over a quarter of a century ago in California.

My former wife, Beth Gray, had spent many years studying metaphysics. She studied to become a minister with the Universal Church of the Master. In November 1973 she took over a chapter of the church as Pastor from an elderly couple in Redwood City, California and renamed it Trinity Metaphysical Center.

In 1973, just before the center opened, I was 56 years old and had been in business for many years, in banking for almost 25 years and with SRI for eight years. On July 7th of that year, following another intuitive prompting, I took a course in Transcendental Meditation, popularly known as TM, a meditation technique involving the silent repetition of a mantra. For me, it was a powerful experience because it led me to realize the existence of other levels of consciousness beyond just waking and sleeping.

In 1973, TM was booming. Many people were being initiated and many groups in the San Francisco Bay area practiced TM together. A group at SRI met in the basement on Wednesdays at lunchtime. I regularly attended that meeting, another at a church on Thursday evenings and any other time I found out there was a meeting. Meditating twice a day, I became proficient in meditation and the practice of well-being. The result of this effort was meditative peacefulness extending into more and more of my activities.

At the time Beth opened her center, I was so involved in work projects at SRI, I was unable to participate in the formation of her church. However, I regularly attended Sunday evening meetings. Beth's typical program included a prayer, a spoken and musical healing meditation, a speaker on a metaphysical topic followed by demonstrations of extra-sensory awareness and a closing prayer.

The healing meditation was intriguing to me. I had no experience with any form of spiritual healing but I enjoyed watching persons who called themselves healers. During the first few months of the church services, three people from the audience would sit on three stools placed in the front of the room. Those who had designated themselves as healers would then deliver the healing as they believed it should be done. Some healers believed one had to touch the body in order to heal it, so their hands would be placed on the body of the person on the stool. Other healers believed one had to heal the aura before the body could be healed, so they held their hands several inches away from the body. Two healers believed that energy came in one hand and out the other hand, so they tucked one hand in back of them and placed the other hand on the person to be healed. One man believed that he had to wave a symbol with one hand while he touched the body with the other hand. Another spoke in tongues while he was healing. The healing meditation was in chaos while he was at the church, which fortunately was only for two weeks.

I observed that about one-third of the healers felt worse at the end of the healing meditation, while there seemed to be little improvement in the health of those who sat for healings.

Beth was planning to discontinue the healing part of the service when a United Airlines Captain named Wally Richardson phoned. He talked about a class in a healing modality called Reiki that he had taken during a stopover in Honolulu. The teacher, Mrs. Hawayo Takata, was coming to visit him in California and would be willing to teach classes while she was in town. He asked if anyone from the church would like to take a class from her at his home.

Beth and several others from the church enrolled in this

first workshop. Several weeks later I enrolled in the second workshop, along with several more people from the church. My attunement for 1st Degree was in Wally Richardson's home on June 12, 1974. I don't remember much of it, except that Takata wore a beautiful gold gown. She was an impressive five-foot, 96-pound Japanese-American woman, whose Hawaiian accent I could hardly understand. But her presence commanded respect.

While I don't recall a great many details, I do know this was highly significant time for me, not only from what I felt as a result of the class, but also from what I heard Mrs. Takata say about the features of Reiki:

- The Reiki system is simple, so simple a child can use it. The practitioner uses a technique of laying on of hands in specific patterns on the body, moving from one position to the next as the hands cool off.
- Practitioners do not use their own energy for healing, but rather become conduits for universal life energy (Reiki).
- The practitioner and the client both feel better after a treatment.
- The practitioner may work on and heal him or herself.
- Practitioners are protected from picking up clients' physical or emotional problems.
- Reiki is an effective modality in emergencies.

All of these points made a deep impression on me. After receiving the basic training in Reiki, I began to participate in the church healing meditation. Later, Beth decided to require all healers to take Reiki before they could participate in the healing meditation. With this change, we observed that the problems in the church's healing program stopped. Healers felt better at the end of the twenty-minute meditation and significant healings began to happen. One man's blood pressure dropped from high to normal. The lumps on one woman's breast disappeared. We continued to require healers to take classes from Takata before they could participate in the healing meditation.

About two weeks after I took the first Reiki class, Beth and I were returning from visiting a friend in a Redwood City hospital. We went to our car in the parking lot where I held the car door open for Beth. When she got in, I closed the door on her hand. When I opened the door, releasing her hand, Beth fainted. I held her inside the car until she recovered consciousness. Then I went around to the driver's side, got in and held her injured hand for about 40 minutes. When the almost unbearable pain subsided, I continued to hold her hand for several minutes more. The pain eased and then went away. When I took my hands away, her hand was completely well, no black and blue. She had flex in her knuckles with only a little black mark on a fingernail. It was as though nothing had happened. This was complete evidence to Beth and me that the system really worked. I knew that Reiki flowed through me even though I was a beginner. This was a point of awakening for me, and the force of that awakening has carried on through the many years.

Beth and I asked Takata, as she liked to be called, if she would give classes at our house in Woodside. She agreed, and on June 12, 1974, we began an association of several years in which she would stay at our house, giving a class or two while she was enroute from Honolulu to visit her daughter in Iowa. She also instructed us informally in Reiki concepts and practices. Takata came frequently, staying a week in the house. A trim, elegant lady, she wore normal western-style clothing, but when teaching she wore beautiful gowns. She stayed in the blue room and ran up horrendous phone bills. She was a vegetarian, enjoying however, from time to time, such non-vegetarian dishes as lamb kidney sautéed in gin (vegetarian lambs of course).

During one of her first Reiki classes at our house, a man with severe multiple sclerosis arrived in his wheel chair. He needed me to write his check for the class fee, signing it with his hand making a fist to grasp the pen. Following the class, he contracted with a student to live at his house, doing the housework and supervising swimming sessions in his pool. He also asked me for Reiki sessions, which I agreed to give him weekly before the meeting at Trinity Center on Sunday. The treatments worked so well that in three months he was able to walk into Trinity Center with a cane and play the piano for us.

This experience led us to give regular treatments before the meeting. Persons who had taken Reiki classes would join me. Takata suggested that we give each recipient an envelope for a donation with "THANKS TO REIKI" printed on it. This was the beginning of the first and largest American Reiki Center, and it lasted for many years. I supervised the Sunday sessions from 1974 to 1979, when I eventually became a minister in the Universal Church of the Master. The number of sessions grew so that when I left in 1979, we had ten bodywork tables for ten people to receive treatments at the same time. We usually held two sessions before the Church service began, so 20 people could receive Reiki, with between 10 and 35 Reiki practitioners giving the sessions. Mrs. Takata helped us to set up and supervise the sessions. During this time from 1974 to January 1979, my day work was with the Bechtel Power Company, in its planning and scheduling system.

In 1975, at the age of 74, Takata suffered a severe heart attack in Honolulu. At first, we did not know about it and accepted her explanation that she had fallen from a ladder. Following her recovery she considered retirement but she was kept from doing so by realizing that she was the only person in the world who could teach Reiki. In 1976, on her next visit to Woodside from Honolulu, she invited me with a few others to become instructors. I, of course, said yes, because I wanted to continue supplying Reiki practitioners for the Sunday church service at Trinity Center.

I became a Reiki Master, on October 6, 1976. I was the third master Takata trained. One of the three, Virginia Samdahl has since died, and the other, Ethel Lombardi, is no longer actively teaching Reiki. Thus, I am currently the longest continuously practicing Reiki Master in the West.

Takata wrote the following Christmas holiday letter to friends and colleagues in 1977, acknowledging that she was passing on the Reiki tradition:

> "Seasons Greetings for a Happy Prosperous 1977. I wish to thank you all for the many kindnesses given me, with gifts, bouquets, invitations to your lovely homes to share the feasts you so kindly prepared with Love and Reiki Hands.
>
> It is with gratitude and Aloha to you all that I write this letter to say "Thank You," to let you know that the time has come for me to retire this year. I have gained many friends and students during my Reiki Tours these past years. They were a great joy, inspiring receiving knowledge and Wisdom.
>
> I have created three Reiki Masters to carry on this noble work. They are trusting, capable, kind, and with humility serve God and mankind. They are: Master John Gray, California; Master Virginia Samdahl, Illinois; Master Ethel Lombardi, Illinois.
>
> I remain, most gratefully yours,
> Rev. Hawayo Takata"

Takata gives a Reiki session to John Harvey Gray

In 1979, I left the business world altogether and began to practice and teach Reiki full time. The first year was a dreadful time. I did not earn enough money and worried that I would have to go back to business. I offered treatments and presented workshops primarily around the San Francisco area but also traveled to teach in Washington State, New York City, Virginia, and New Hampshire.

In 1984, I moved to Ruckersville, Virginia, about 10 miles north of Charlottesville, having heard the call, "Move east, young man." I rented a little house in the country and settled in, but I never really established a practice there. The next year, I moved to the Boston area and have been in the northeast ever since. I lived in Concord, Watertown, Marblehead, and Gloucester Massachusetts, and now live comfortably with Lourdes in a lovely, cozy house in Rindge, New Hampshire, with room for healing and teaching.

In 1994, Interface, the popular holistic health learning

center in Cambridge, Massachusetts, voted me Teacher of the Year. My students continue to open Reiki wellness centers and Lourdes and I started one at our home in Rindge during the spring of 1998. It is gratifying to see academic institutions give credit for Reiki training, and more and more hospitals encouraging the practice of Reiki as a complement to allopathic medicine for the greater benefit of their patients.

So, that curiosity about hands-on healing way back in 1974 changed my life. I have been giving workshops for 25 years and finished my 740th class as of July 2001, each class lasting from two to five days. My style of Reiki, what I term the Usui-Gray Integrated System, includes meditation, scanning the aura and the chakras, and looking for the breaks in the aura, which I call "zings." More on all that in chapters to come.

After receiving my mastership, I had three more experiences which enriched my road to healing.

Being born overseas and living abroad for my first ten years, I was comfortable thinking about other countries, and interested in other ways of living and being. I explored the Hindu method of working with mantras. With a friend in 1981, I practiced Siddha Yoga at an ashram near Oakland. The experience surprised me because the group sang in Sanskrit with the women sitting separate from the men. These bells and whistles didn't remind me of any religious experience, but I was interested in the calm and peacefulness that people who practice Siddha Yoga seemed to exhibit. To stay alert on long auto trips, I started to sing the popular mantra "Om Namah Shivaya" to keep me awake.

In 1983, I taught a couple of Reiki workshops in State College, Pennsylvania. I stayed with a professor of psychology at Pennsylvania State University who practiced with Swami Rama, an Indian yogi master, with an ashram in Honesdale, Pennsylvania. I had read about Swami Rama in a book called, *Beyond Biofeedback* by Elmer and Alyse Green.

They recounted how Swami Rama used two types of mantras, one to elicit a peaceful state and the other to elicit an excitatory state. The Greens described how Swami Rama used the power of thought to move an object suspended by a string several feet away. He would begin to mutter an excitatory mantra to himself the day before, to prepare for this.

I went to the ashram for a week's vacation from traveling around the country giving workshops. It was a peaceful, gentle ashram that did a lot of yoga. I was only peripherally interested, but I did practice yoga.

My experience with Siddha Yoga shifted my emotional set-point to a more relaxed, trusting and peaceful state. I still had an interest in future events but not a fixation. I also became interested in the experience of dying and the possibility of other lives that we may have had in the past or would have in the future.

I also read a book about Sai Baba, a Hindu holy man. In India, people consider him to be a representative of God, like the Buddha, Christ or Krishna. I thought it would be interesting to visit Sai Baba so he could help me to improve my ability to transmit Reiki.

Soon after, two friends, Tim and Jane, invited me to give a Reiki workshop at their home in Charlotte, Vermont. When I entered the room in which I was to stay, I saw a photo of Sai Baba. I immediately ran downstairs to ask Jane about it. She told me, "Yes, I that is Sai Baba. I visited his ashrams in Puttaparthi, India."

When I asked her if she had stayed for some time, she answered, "I was on a tour of India and was only planning two or three days there." "But," I said, "You stayed a year." She responded, "That's right. I stayed longer in India than I thought I would. Is there anything else that you can tell me about myself?" I had run out of intuition and had nothing to add.

Toward morning, in the bedroom with the picture, I had

the experience of feeling that my head was taken off and then put back on the way it should be, perhaps so I could be a better channel for Reiki.

When I told a friend, Kathleen Curry, back in Virginia about the experience, I said that it triggered the thought that I would take a trip to India. She replied, "I'm going too."

Kathleen and I selected a time a couple of months away. Since my daughter worked with a group that had designed, built and was operating the Hotel Vajra in Kathmandu, Nepal, I wanted to see it as well as staying at Sai Baba's ashram.

After a tour around Kathmandu, we flew to New Delhi, then to Bangalore. We were billeted at a hotel which was primarily concerned with Sai Baba, so the next day, the manager of the hotel got a taxi for Kathleen and me for Puttaparthi, where Sai Baba resides.

We drove 100 miles northwest of Bangalore to Puttaparthi, through small Indian villages which, in my mind, were quite squalid, and dry country with desert-like vegetation even in places being farmed. When we reached the entrance to the ashram, suddenly everything changed. We passed several well-built schools with statues of Indian deities beautiful in blue and pink.

When we checked in, people made certain we were visitors, not Indian, and separated us. Kathleen went to a large shed with other women and I went to a men's shed with about 100 beds. There I rented a mattress from a person outside the ashram. He brought it in for me, but I made my own bed. Across the aisle I recognized a man who lived in a town about five miles away from Woodside, California who had worked at Stanford Research Institute during the same nine years I did. We chatted and traded information.

There were quite a few foreigners besides me, meaning, people who were not Indian. We ate in the foreigners' dining room where the food seemed quite spicy to me but, I was told, was much less spicy than the food in the main dining room where the Indians ate.

Bedtime and lights out was at 9:00 p.m. We were awakened at 3:30 a.m. for a walking meditation. When breakfast was over, there was darshan, a time set aside to see an ashram's leader or guru. Darshan was held in the temple yard. Everyone stood in one of the 20 to 25 lines in the courtyard. The person at the head of each line reached into a worker's pouch and pulled out a number. Number One was lucky because line one moved first. I got into line one three times out of the twenty I went to darshan, quite an extraordinary number.

At the appointed time, Sai Baba walked out of the temple where he lived on the second floor, first to the women's area and then to the men's area. Sai Baba is a little man, about five feet tall with high bushy hair that elevates him about four inches. As he walked along the front of the line, people held out a letter or letters for him to take. I was holding three or four letters I brought from home and one I wrote while I was there, telling him that I wanted to be a better channel for Reiki. As he walked by, he looked into my eyes. His were fathomless. It is said that he knows everything about you from birth until death and I felt that. He didn't take the letters. What he said to me without speaking was "Ha, here you're trying to give me a letter and you've forgotten what was in the letter." I accepted that explanation and went back and memorized my letter. A few days later, I was again in the first row of line one and held out my letters. This time, he took them without looking at me. He normally invites five to ten people into the temple for an interview. I never got an interview, which was all right.

Once I saw him manifesting *Vhibuti*, which is a form of ash materialized from thin air. Sai Baba does this by rotating his hand, tipping it over and dropping the Vhibuti into the hand. This happened ten yards from me and was given to an Indian who fell to his knees in thanks.

While I was there, it was rumored that Sai Baba was going to one of his ashrams near Bangalore. When he finally left, most of the people visiting the ashram, almost 3,000 of them, left too. I decided not to go. Kathleen had already gone home, so I stayed at the ashram, going into the temple whenever I could for the ceremonies. The energy was strong because Sai Baba lived upstairs. I got a feeling for the ashram, the energy around it and a feeling for Sai Baba. I believe my energy increased greatly from my experience with Sai Baba and made me better channeler of Reiki.

My experiences with transcendental meditation, with Siddha Yoga at Swami Rama's Himalayan Institute and with Sai Baba's ashram, seem to tie together. In each place I came to a more peaceful way of living. I overcame my anxiety about the future. My emotional set-point is now much more peaceful than it was. As a result, I am a more effective healer.

Chapter 2
Lourdes' Story

I was born in Camaguey, Cuba in March of 1954. I came from a family of wealthy cattle ranchers. My mother, Adriana Cervantes, was 42 years old at the time, and already had a son, 13, and daughter, 12. When she became pregnant with me the doctors advised her to have an abortion, because it was risky back then for a woman of her age to give birth. Chances were, the doctors told her, that I would have problems, and her own well-being could be imperiled. My father was frightened, and advised my mother to have an abortion. Abortion was not a raging public issue in those days. My family was flexible enough that she could probably have gone ahead with the abortion, and it wouldn't have been a big issue. The big issue was my mother's safety. But she was adamant: she would have the baby. That is how I came to be born.

My mother named me Mary of Lourdes, Maria de Lourdes, even before I was born, for healing and compassion were her devotion. She was wholly devoted to the healing of Lourdes, and to healing in general. The devotion to the healing of Lourdes dates back to 1858 when a 14-year-old girl named Bernadette Soubirous from the town of Lourdes, France, saw visions of the Virgin Mary standing by a stream. The Virgin revealed her identity to the girl and indicated to her the healing properties coming from the waters. Skeptical at first, the Catholic Church eventually declared the authenticity of Bernadette's visions. Today, Lourdes is a major pilgrimage center with over 3,000,000 visitors per year, including approximately 50,000 sick and disabled, looking for miraculous healing. While Mary of Lourdes was my mother's devotion, it is not especially mine, though like her I am wholeheartedly devoted to healing. I subscribe to no one particular faith; rather, I seek insights from a wide range of religions and beliefs. To me, it does not matter where the insights come from—Christianity, Buddhism, Judaism, Hinduism, or somewhere else. I believe in a Divine Intelligence which governs the Universe. Reiki—Universal Life Force—is a manifestation of this Divinity. It matters not whether it is called Ki, Prana, Qi, or Holy Spirit. It is the same.

I understand that our actions are the true expressions of our faith. Our actions—not just our words—are what really count. I often reflect on the words of Paul Hawken in his book, *The Ecology of Commerce.* He wrote: "Leave the world better than you found it. Take no more than you need. Try not to harm life or the environment. Make amends if you do."

As a little girl, one of my first presents was a saddle. My father, Rafael Cervantes, had me riding before I was three years old. I could ride better than I could walk. I loved the country and the animals.

I had a baby lamb. I raised a rooster, a fighting cock, from an egg. He followed me around thinking that I was his mother. He wouldn't let anybody else near.

For as long as I can remember, my mother used to do charitable work. Being wealthy, we had servants. My mother had her own chauffeur and I had my own nanny. But I never saw my mother, Adriana, at a country club. That wasn't her style.

There was no welfare in Cuba in the 1940s and 50's, back in the days of Fulgencio Batista. When impoverished persons became ill and couldn't work, there was literally no one to help them. Unless charities came into aid them, their families went hungry. No formal social mechanism alleviated the sufferings of the poor. Cuba was a two-class society in those days. You were either rich, or you were poor.

If my mother found that a destitute person needed medical attention, she brought the doctor and paid for his services. She always provided as much assistance as she could. My mother and a friend, Rita Maria, were the head honchos, if you will, in collecting clothing, funds, food, medicines, whatever and delivering it to the poor. All of that made a deep impression on me.

In Cuba we had country healers using herbs and different forms of energy to heal. I grew up in that environment helping and being aware of other alternative forms of healing. Consequently, I developed great curiosity and love for the mystery of energy flow.

My family suffered greatly from communism. They were devastated—my father in particular—when the communists took over our properties. With my parents, I came to America in 1966. The Cuban government allowed us to take with us only one pair of shoes and two changes of clothes each— everything else was left behind. When we arrived in Miami, U. S. Immigration gave us a $20 bill, a handshake, and a wish of good luck. That was it. Here we were in America.

At 12 years of age I experienced a drastic change from a Cuban lifestyle to an American one. It was quite a come down from having a house with servants and wealth, where we could enjoy luxuries. Suddenly we were here and everything was different. My father was heartsick, and so was my mother, because my sister was still in Cuba. Her husband was of military age, and the Cuban government would not permit them to leave the country. Then there was the new language and culture. We settled in Northern Virginia, where my brother was already located.

I attended a small Catholic school with no program for English as a second language and no other Hispanic people. I learned English with a dictionary. I had no one of my own culture to be with day to day. I struggled to learn English and keep up with the class.

All of us have had experiences growing up that were significant and even traumatic. I no longer had my home, my country, my language, or even my horse. Coming from Cuba and going through this complete shift from riches to rags I developed an emotional set-point of loneliness. I even felt separated from my parents who were mourning their losses and were terrified for the safety of my sister and her family. In a communist country you can be arrested for no reason.

I grew up with all that in the background—sensing, feeling, sometimes hearing my mother articulate her concerns and worries, and being acutely aware of my father's silence (which is how he coped with grief). I felt isolated, and that created a set-point of sadness. I now understand that a weak throat chakra (energy center) relates to a set-point of sadness and separation.

My throat chakra was low for a long time and I suffered from frequent respiratory infections, but since I started doing Reiki, I have not had a cold or flu. Any time I feel a scratchy throat or cough, I do what John suggests, which is to go to bed, rest and start doing a Reiki self-treatment. Then, I drift off to sleep for a nap with the Reiki energy still flowing through my hands. By the time I wake up, I'm fine. It never fails.

I married young and had a son, Joe. I later became divorced and Joe and I were on our own. Later, I studied Hapkido, a Korean martial art with Jun Saeng Yoo, a Korean

Grandmaster and Eighth Degree black belt. I will always be grateful to Mr. Yoo, "Kwan Jang Nim,"(grandmaster in Korean) for his teachings of righteousness, courtesy and patience; these have made a significant impact in my life.

At the time I first took Reiki in 1994 I was heavily engaged in business. I ran a mortgage loan origination office in Northern Virginia, focused on refinancing homes, and was busy seven days a week. I didn't have much free time that summer, certainly not to go away on vacation, and felt generally tired and stressed. I had a one weekend off and decided to take a Reiki class. This literally changed my life. From the moment I was attuned, I could feel the flow of energy. I was already familiar with the use of ki because of my martial arts training and very aware of what was happening. I found Reiki fascinating and started doing treatments right away. I fell in love with Reiki and wanted to learn everything that I could.

I took my first Reiki course from a man named John Veltheim from Australia. He happened to be touring the US and taught a class in the Washington, DC area. The class was good and I enjoyed it.

Right away I discovered the therapeutic benefits of falling asleep while touching my own body. You see, Reiki flows even after you are asleep as long as you keep your hands in contact with your body. This touch also creates a very soothing and comforting sensation. I often woke with my bedclothes soaked in perspiration produced by the Reiki energy and had a menstrual period lasting two weeks—this was all part of a profound cleansing, or purification process. Before Reiki, I suffered from chronic back pain; my shoulders were as hard as rocks. Massage didn't relax them. With Reiki, in about six months my back felt fine. Reiki's greatest benefit for me, however, was how it helped to change my personality from being a nervous, anxious, sad person to a much more relaxed, calm, and happy one.

After taking that first class with John Veltheim, I kept

studying and researching. I'd had such a powerful, life-changing experience with Reiki I, that I felt with certainty that there was more. Then when I saw John Harvey Gray's name the first time, something struck me. I knew that I had just seen something significant and had a feeling that it was important. I needed to go see John. I wanted to know more about Reiki and wanted to go back to the roots of the practice. I wanted to study with him, to get as close to the source of the teachings as I could. That's when I called him. He was living in Gloucester, Massachusetts at the time. I told him that I wanted to be a Reiki Master and wanted to learn all that I could about the energy. But John was firm. He said "wait, hold off a minute. Let's not go this fast. You will have to study with me, starting over with Reiki I and then I will have to make an assessment of your qualifications and so forth. " I asked him when he was teaching his next class. It was November of 1994 and he said he would be in the Washington DC area next spring. I said, "No, no, when is your next class?" John said that he would be teaching in Gloucester the very next weekend. I responded immediately: "I'll be there."

I took the train up to Boston and John graciously agreed to pick me up at South Station. He said, "look for the man wearing a black beret. " We found each other at the train station and he helped me carry my luggage out to his car, a white Saturn station wagon, with a license plate that said "Reiki Master. " We quickly drove up to where he was living, in the old seaport city of Gloucester. On the way we chatted pleasantries. He took me to a beautiful old hotel within walking distance of his home, and said he would pick me up in an hour for dinner. I freshened up and in an hour he was there. He took me to a very nice restaurant where we ate.

I was trying to find out more about him at dinner. What I could get out of John, at that point, without being a close friend, was not much. He's very private, and doesn't like to get into personal conversations with people he has just met. I was trying to walk the fine line between being pleasant, talking in depth with this man who absolutely fascinated me, and finding out more about Reiki, which was already a passion in my life.

Hawayo Takata did not spend equal amounts of time with all the Reiki Masters she trained. She wanted to be sure the legacy of Reiki would survive and knew that she was growing older and was running out of time. She needed to create masters quickly. She had much more time to spend with the Masters she trained first. With John, and his first wife, Beth, Takata spent weeks living at their home in California. She had her own bedroom in their house. John got to talk, study and practice with Takata every day for weeks at a time.

John has found a universe of differences between what he teaches—what he received from Takata—and what Reiki has become in the wide world. You have to remember that many people changed Reiki. Being an oral tradition, it is very vulnerable to change. So now John has a hard and fast rule, if you want to study with him, you start from the beginning.

Eventually, John and I became great friends. There was something about John. Even though I loved what I got out of the previous Reiki class, this was different. I had finally found the right teacher. But something else happened. I remember going home to Virginia and telling a friend about John, that he was the kind of man I wanted to be with: sensitive and funny, down to earth, not pretentious, very deep. I was comfortable with him, talking with him. I knew that I could talk with him about anything and be understood, be listened to, that we could share. And we did, sometimes talking for hours in the middle of the night on the phone, between Virginia and Gloucester. It was as though we had been together always. It was that kind of beautiful chemistry.

John tells me he always knew that this was my life's work.

I remember him saying to me, "I will teach you all I know. " The first thing he had me do was work with the energy, as a daily practice, a meditation. I still work with the energy daily, and always will, because I continue to learn from it. The knowledge unfolds and presents itself to me as I give myself to this daily practice.

John taught me to be one with the Reiki energy without trying to control it. I don't have to do anything. All I have to do is observe. It will show me what to do if I just listen and come to a still point—to surrender. So often, we want to be powerful and loved and accepted, and we try to control. If we simply surrender and trust, the Reiki energy will teach us. It will show us exactly what we need.

John doesn't teach with a lot of words. Without saying anything, he has you experience the lesson kinesthetically, whatever it may be. I know from my experience and from other students of his, that John might not be saying a word, but he communicates in a way that the message is felt and understood and becomes a part of you. He doesn't try to teach you on some schedule. It becomes an unfolding process, like packets of information planted in my soul and the soul of his students, ready to open up like little Christmas gifts when we are prepared to know and accept the lesson.

John works in an intuitive way to help students develop their own intuition. I call his work Intuitive Reiki. John doesn't put on any airs, nor have a big ego about who he is and what he has done in the world. He doesn't beat his chest and say "I am better, I have done this," or become inaccessible to those who want to learn from him. He doesn't put himself up on a pedestal. One of the things that struck me when I met John, was how accessible he was to others, to students and how he could communicate at a level that each student could quickly grasp.

After I took my first class with John, I began to volunteer. I wanted to keep exploring this wonderful healing gift in depth. Reading the newspaper at home one day, I noticed an ad. The Whitman-Walker clinic in Arlington, Virginia, just outside Washington, D. C., was looking for Reiki practitioners to work on HIV and AIDS patients. "Yippee!" I said. "Here I come!"

At the clinic, I received training on how to work there. Then I started volunteering one day a week, as many sessions as I could possibly do. Touching someone and connecting with them, knowing that I was part of a process, a channel for this healing energy and love, was important to me. The more I did it, the more I loved it. The more nurturance I felt from the energy, the more appreciation I experienced from the people that I treated. For me, that was the "Aha" experience of Reiki. It was unconditional love. I thought, "This is what I have been searching for!"

I began working with a man at the clinic named Teddy. He had full-blown AIDS, which he had contracted from an infected needle. He was also an alcoholic and drug addict. Teddy's liver was so damaged that his body could no longer handle medication. He was in constant agony. When I gave him his first session, he felt immediate relief. Teddy and I soon decided that since the only way he could feel any comfort was through Reiki, I would come to his home every night, seven nights a week, after I finished work at the mortgage company, and give him a treatment.

At the same time, I got my first massage table from the mother of a young man who had just died of AIDS. She wanted me to use it to help other AIDS patients. So, I took it over to Teddy's house and left it there. In less than two weeks *daily* Teddy's pain disappeared. By the end of two months, his liver was well enough to be put back on medication. His T-cell count was way up.

I got confirmation right away. I loved it. I wanted to dedicate myself even more to healing. I felt connected. This was my way of healing my own emotional set-point of loneliness and separation. I remember saying to my friends and myself, "I don't feel alone anymore."

I grabbed everyone who would let me and gave them a Reiki session. I was fortunate, because my friends were receptive. They loved it, wanted and were happy to receive it. That is how I learned. I went beyond the training I received in a class. I practiced it.

One of my responsibilities at the mortgage company where I was working was to train new loan officers. I enjoyed doing this so much. I knew that if I combined Reiki with teaching, this would be my true calling.

I continued training with John, traveling North regularly for many weekends. I would either fly into Boston, or ride the Amtrak train from Washington to Boston's South Station. During the day, I assisted John at his Reiki workshops. Nights were just for us.

Then one day, John asked, "Would you marry me?" I fell silent, completely dumbfounded. I wasn't expecting that question. I took two days to muster up the courage to say "yes. " I am so happy that I did.

We are nearly 40 years apart in age. It seems like a big gap, but together, our souls are the same age. We play, we laugh, we share, we have the same sense of humor. We were the perfect combination, and I knew it from the moment we met. It was not because he was John Harvey Gray the Reiki Master, it was because he is just John, and we had the right chemistry.

After two years of intensive study, John knew that I was ready. He trained me to become a Reiki Master Instructor. I completed this training in October, 1996. Mastership felt overwhelming at first. I was exhausted because, as I have later learned, new masters have a tendency to use their own energy in attunements, and we were teaching every week. After the workshops, I would come home and have to lie down.

What first brought me to Reiki was my connection to unconditional love. Suddenly, through my hands, I could give love to any person, animal, or plant that needed help and healing. I could, through Reiki energy, love them and receive love back. My first experience of the efficacy and importance of Reiki had come from the heart. This will always come first with me. But eventually, I wanted to learn more to satisfy the demands of my mind.

I decided to do some research. I discovered that the human energy field and the energy centers of the body are not just theoretical. They are real. We experience them through our direct senses when we do Reiki, but they are also well documented in scientific literature. Harold Saxon Burr, Professor of Neuroanatomy at the Yale University School of Medicine, began some key scientific work on this subject in the 1940s by studying the pattern of energy fields surrounding living things. He called them L-fields, or "fields of life." He was fascinated with these energy fields, and wanted to know as much as he could about them.

Dr. Burr was convinced that energy fields are the basic blueprints for all life. He believed that every physiological process has an electrical counterpart, and because of this, diseases alter energy fields before visible pathological changes, such as tumors, begin. If the disturbed energy field could be detected and restored to normal, the sickness could be prevented.

I found the work of Burr and many other scientists carefully documented and collected in some wonderful books by James L. , Oschman, Ph. D. and his wife Nora. In particular, I enjoyed *Readings on the Scientific Basis of Bodywork, Energetic, and Movement Therapies*, and *What is 'Healing Energy'? The Scientific Basis of Energy Medicine*. These books have greatly deepened my understanding and appreciation of how healing energy actually works.

Oschman also wrote of the discoveries of Nobel Price

winner Albert Szent-Gyorgyi who discovered that the proteins in the human body act as semiconductors. Szent-Gyorgyi concluded in 1941 that virtually all of the molecules that form living tissue are capable of transporting energy. This was a profoundly important insight for me because it helped me to understand how energy moves in the body.

Because of this, I realized that these subtle energy systems are not just in the body, but in every living thing on our planet. That is why John and I regularly offer Reiki to the Earth. We observe the condition of the Earth and see the pollution and disrespect. We believe that the health of the Earth and its energy systems are largely disregarded. The air, the water and the soil are being exploited and poisoned, threatening the balance of natural systems for our children and grandchildren. We want this to change and we hope that every Reiki practitioner will want this too.

Because we believe this, we remain properly informed on ecological issues and the role that businesses and government truly play. For example, if every person in America recycled their trash, it would only amount to 2% of the total pollution created, because 98% of the pollution is created by business. What we do in our personal lives is just not enough. So, we support businesses that are ecologically oriented and that do not destroy the environment. When we buy a product, we think about its true cost; not just what is coming out of our pockets now, but how much it will cost in the long run. We vote for the people who will implement policies that protect wildlife and natural resources. We believe that our lives, and all life on Earth, depend on this.

I believe that a quiet state of mind is very important for Reiki students to achieve. This is a place of profoundly relaxed awareness and is conveyed to your client directly through your hands. People want to know how and why John's Reiki sessions are so powerful. I would say that he knows how to quiet his mind. John is in that peaceful state all the time, especially when he is doing a treatment, a high contrast to his mental and emotional state 25 years ago when he was a businessman in a constant state of anxiety. John has said to me that meditation saved his life. If he hadn't started Transcendental Meditation back in 1973 and then had the courage to follow his soul path to become a wonderful healer and teacher, he says he would not be alive now.

666-GRAY

Chapter 3
The Recovery of Reiki

Mrs. Hawayo Takata brought Reiki to the United States, first by way of Hawaii in the late-1930s and then California, in the mid-1970s. In all of her workshops, she shared a story of how Dr. Mikao Usui rediscovered and developed Reiki. She said that Dr. Usui was Rector at Doshisha University in Kyoto, Japan late in the 19th Century, and that his quest to recover Reiki was prompted by a question about the Bible.

Recent research by Frank Arjava Petter in his book, *Reiki Fire*, demonstrates that some parts of the story—such as where Mikao Usui went to school, where he taught, and his religious orientation are inaccurate. Takata's story is a teaching story, intended to convey certain lessons. Because this story has impelled the development of Reiki in the West, and because we feel it offers worthwhile lessons for all along the Reiki path, we tell this story the same way Takata told it to John.

The story starts on a Sunday morning when Dr. Usui was conducting a question and answer session with his students at Doshisha University. One student in the front row raised his hand. Dr. Usui said, "Yes, what is it?"

The student said, "We here in the front row have been talking about the Bible and we wonder if the events in the Bible are true?"

Dr. Usui said, "Oh, sure, the events in the Bible and particularly in the New Testament, are about a tribe of Middle Eastern people. The Bible chronicles the events in their lives. Yes, it is very true."

The student said, "What do you think about the New Testament? Do you think what is written about Jesus is true?"

Dr. Usui said, "Yes, Jesus experienced all the situations described in the New Testament."

The student asked, "Like healing the blind and the lame and walking on water?"

Dr. Usui said, "Yes, he could do such things."

"Well then," said the student, "how about a demonstration, Dr. Usui?" Dr. Usui fell silent. After several minutes, he said, "I don't know how Jesus could perform miraculous healings, let alone walk on water. I only know what was taught to me in the seminary in Japan where I took my Christian training. I am going to step down as Rector of Doshisha University and go to a country that is more predominantly Christian and study Christianity in depth. When I learn how Jesus could do those things, then I will come back and tell you."

That was probably the last that Doshisha University saw of Dr. Usui, because in a few weeks he was on board a steamer bound for the United States. Takata did not give the particulars about why he chose to enroll at the University of Chicago, but that is where he went to school.

First, Usui studied English so he could communicate in this new land. Then, he studied Jesus and The Bible. Usui was an astute, intelligent and sensitive man. He probably memorized large portions of the Bible and read all the documents and manuscripts that he could find about Jesus. He must have buttonholed people with authoritative information hoping to find out more about how Jesus could perform miraculous healings and walk on water.

His studies of Christianity uncovered no clues as to how Jesus could perform such miracles, but instead led him to research comparative religion for several years.

Eventually, he discovered that Gautama Buddha could perform similar healings of the blind, lame and leprous. Since Japan is predominantly Buddhist, he returned there to try to unearth the Buddha's system for healing. Usui decided to stay in a Buddhist temple while undergoing his studies.

In Buddhism, just as in the other great religions, different sects and denominations exist. Usui walked from temple to temple searching for the right one to live in. He always asked the head monk at each temple if he believed the Buddha could perform miraculous healings. The head monk invariably said he believed the Buddha could do such things, but now they were more concerned with the spiritual aspects of people who came to them for help. They left physical healings to doctors, who have nurses and hospitals.

Usui finally came to a Zen Buddhist temple in Kyoto. The head monk, an old man with a sweet voice and kindly face, greeted him. In response to Dr. Usui's question, he replied that he believed Buddha could perform miraculous healings, but did not know how. The monk explained the Zen belief that upon reaching the highest level of meditation, many things will be made known, including how the Buddha could perform miraculous healings. Since this was the only temple that gave him encouragement in his search, Usui took a room there, ate his meals, took hot baths and worked on his studies.

Dr. Usui studied Japanese texts, documents, manuscripts and scriptures on Buddhism. He consulted people with authoritative information about Gautama Buddha. After a long time, he realized that he still did not know how the Buddha could perform healings. Knowing that Buddhism originated in the northwest of India and came to Japan following many years in China, he decided to read Chinese documents. Chinese was another language to learn. In time, after learning Chinese and reading the Chinese translations of the Sutras, Usui recognized that he still did not know how the Buddha performed healings.

Usui felt perplexed. He thought to himself, "Perhaps the problem lies with the Japanese and Chinese manuscripts. Could it be that these later translations do not reflect the exact meaning of the original Sanskrit texts?" So, Usui undertook and mastered the study of Sanskrit. After years of study, he found a Buddhist Sutra (story) that had a passage about healing which was clear to him as a mathematical formula about how Buddha could perform healings. Many formulae are structured in a format such as a + b = c. For the formula to be useful, one must know what the components "a" and "b" represent.

Dr. Mikao Usui (1864-1926)

Dr. Usui had finally uncovered the Buddha's formula for healing but did not understand how to use it. There were no instructions! Remembering the words of the old monk " . . . upon reaching the highest level of meditation, many things will be made known . . ." he decided to climb Mount Kurayama, some 17 miles outside Kyoto, and meditate for as long as three weeks on how to use the formula.

He took leave of the old monk in the Zen temple, telling him to please send a search party after him if he was not back in 21 days. Usui climbed to an auspicious spot on Kurayama where he spread his cloak upon the ground and gathered 21 pebbles. He planned to throw one pebble away each day so he would know how many days were left. He began his meditation, fasting from everything but water. The meditation progressed and the pebbles dwindled.

When one pebble was left, during the darkest part of the night before dawn, Usui beheld a flickering light in the distance at about his altitude. It looked like a candle. He watched it with curiosity wondering what it was. It seemed to be approaching the mountain. Suddenly, he realized it was coming straight for him. He stood up and braced himself, ready for whatever consequences. The flame of light rushed at him and struck him on the forehead. He fell over backward, unconscious.

When Usui recovered consciousness and sat up, before him as if on a screen were myriads of different-colored lighted bubbles dancing along. The bubbles stopped. As he looked at them he could see a symbol. As he memorized the symbol, instruction on its use was conveyed to him. As soon as he memorized it, the bubbles danced again and stopped. Another symbol appeared, he memorized it and the use of the new symbol was conveyed to him. This happened several more times. Finally, when the last symbol disappeared, the screen faded away and his mission on the mountain was complete.

As the light from the new day was coming into the sky, Usui gathered his things together and started back to the monastery in Kyoto. He was not hungry. He felt as satisfied as if he had eaten a large meal the evening before. He thought of this as a miracle.

On the path down the mountain, his foot struck a large stone, taking off half of the toenail of the big toe. It was bleeding badly and so he squatted down and held his toe with his hands thinking to himself, "I am hurt." He held the toe for many minutes and the pain welled up, evened off, and then receded. When he took his hands away, the toenail was firmly back on the toe with the bleeding completely stopped. He experienced this as another miracle. He put his sandals back on and continued on his way.

As the sun was coming into the sky, Usui came to a clearing where he saw a bench covered with a red blanket. In Japan, this is a sign that a small eating-place is nearby. Sure enough, in the corner of the clearing was the snack bar owner, blowing on the coals to start the pot of water on the grate boiling so he could make tea. Dr. Usui asked if there was any cold rice left over from last night's dinner. The snack bar owner answered that there was. Dr. Usui said, "When the tea is done, please bring me tea, rice, salted plums and salted cabbage." The snack bar owner looked at Dr. Usui and said, "From the length of the whiskers on your face, I can see that you have been meditating on the mountain for many days. When I feed people like you, they get a terrible stomach-ache. Instead, I will mash rice into tea, and feed it to you spoonful by spoonful. In several hours you will be on your way." Dr. Usui knew that he did not have that much time because by the end of the day the search party would be looking for him. He told the snack bar owner that he would take responsibility for his own stomach and to please bring him the food when it was ready.

A short while later, the daughter of the snack-bar owner brought him his breakfast. She had a scarf wrapped around her face and was weeping. When Dr. Usui asked her what was wrong, she explained that for the last three days she had a raging toothache but could not go into town to see the doctor because her mother was away and no one else could help her father tend to the eating-place.

Dr. Usui said, "Maybe I can help you." He placed his hands on her face and jaw. After several minutes she broke into a broad smile. Her pain was gone. The girl's father thanked Dr. Usui by saying, "The meal is the house." Dr. Usui thanked him but left coins anyway because he was certain not many travelers came by that way.

Dr. Usui suffered no ill effects from the large meal following his long fast. He arrived at the Zen temple just before nightfall. The pageboy who let him in at the gate was overjoyed to see him because the search party was already forming. After a hot bath and dinner, Dr. Usui paid a visit to the old monk. He was in his room with a terrible backache. As Dr. Usui recounted the events of the last three weeks, he laid his hands along the old monk's spine. Gradually, the pain went away.

Over the next few days, Dr. Usui treated the old monk until he was well again. They discussed how his discovery on the mountain could be brought to the attention of Japan. It was decided that Dr. Usui should move to the largest and poorest slum outside Kyoto. Once there, he would treat the inhabitants one by one. When each inhabitant was made well, he or she would be sent to the old monk, who would give the person a new name, new clothes and a job.

Dr. Usui dressed himself as a vegetable peddler, shouldered a pole with a basket of vegetables at each end and walked to the slum. When he asked the first person he met to whom he should speak to gain permission to stay, he was led to the home of the local "slum boss." The slum boss came out of the hut and looked Dr. Usui up and down. Dr. Usui said to him, "I would like to live here. Please give me permission to stay." The slum boss grunted, "That would be possible, but first you will need to undergo an initiation. Would you be willing to do that?" Dr. Usui agreed. The slum boss said, "To start with, I'll take those baskets of vegetables for myself." And he did. Then, he ordered Usui to take off all his clothes. Dr. Usui did so. Around his waist was a money belt. "Give that to me!" the slum boss demanded. Dr. Usui calmly gave the ruffian his money belt. The slum boss kept all the money except for a few coins, which he distributed to his friends who were watching. Then he pointed to a pile of dirty clothes. A man came over, selected the dirtiest and smelliest of the clothes and tossed them to Dr. Usui, who put them on. The slum boss smirked, "Now you're one of us!" Holding his head high, Dr. Usui turned to him and said, "I will not beg. Please find me an empty hut and from before daylight until after dark I will treat the inhabitants of this slum."

Following the reasoning that the youngest of the adults should be treated first, since their problems would be less chronic, Dr. Usui began his work. He treated the residents of the slum one by one. As each person was cured of physical problems, Dr. Usui sent him or her to the old monk at the temple to receive new clothes, a new name and a job.

After several years, Dr. Usui guessed that by now the slum must be almost empty. He stopped work early one day to wander around the neighborhood. Everyone he saw seemed familiar. He approached a group and asked if he had met them before. They answered, "Don't you remember, Dr. Usui? We were among the first you treated." Dr. Usui asked if they had been sent to the old monk in the Zen temple. Were they not given new clothes and a new name? Didn't they have a job? "Oh yes," they said. "But we found it difficult out in the world. We had to earn money for our board and room. We had to work and treat others as we wanted to be treated. We had a difficult time obeying laws. So, we decided to come back here. We can beg good food and clothes from here. We have something over our head at night."

Dr. Usui realized he had been treating people who were without gratitude. None of them had ever thanked him for the things he had done for them. None had given him anything in return, not a loaf of bread, certainly no money, not even an offer to sweep his floor. He decided then that he was never again going to treat those without gratitude. Usui believed that gratitude was essential for true healing. Later, he taught students to always have an "exchange of energy" of some sort before giving Reiki. It would not matter whether it was in the form of money, barter or even prayer. He cautioned them that without gratitude on the part of the recipient, an imbalance is created, which will likely prevent healing.

Shortly after this realization, Dr. Usui left the slum. He searched the cities of Japan for people to work with him. He gathered acolytes by walking down a street during the day carrying a lighted torch. When a person approached him, asking, "Why are you carrying a lighted torch in broad daylight?" Dr. Usui would reply, "I am looking for people of perception like you. Won't you come over to the temple tonight? I'll be giving a talk." As he gathered students to work with him, he established Reiki healing centers throughout Japan.

Before he made his transition, Mikao Usui trained and attuned several people, including Chujiro Hayashi, an officer in Japan's Naval Reserve, as Reiki Masters. Dr. Hayashi was the leader of at least eight full-time Reiki healing centers in Japan. His Reiki practice lasted until the time of his death in 1941. Based on his training with Usui, Hayashi created his own Reiki instruction manual on how to treat specific ailments (see Appendix A).

Takata's Story

It was to Dr. Hayashi's center in Tokyo that Hawayo Takata went for a cure. Born in the Hawaiian Islands in 1899, she became a widow at age twenty-nine. Takata was left penniless, with two young children to support. Looking back much later, in 1975, she told an interviewer from The Times in San Mateo, California, that at that tragic time in her life, her children alone kept her from suicide. "I would look down at their small faces as they slept peacefully. I knew that I could not do that to them. I was their mother and their father."

She went on with her life, but over the following seven

years she was emotionally devastated. One member of her family died each year. By age 35, Takata had developed serious physical problems including asthma, appendicitis, and gallstones.

"I was always a church-going woman and believed in God," Takata said. "One day while contemplating the situation I thought to myself, 'I feel alone in the world, as if I alone have all the suffering, burdens and poverty.' I asked, 'Why am I poor?' 'Why do I have such illness and pain?' 'Why do I have all the sorrows?' Then Takata prayed, 'God, I am up against the wall. Help me.' She said to herself, "if God hears, He will help."

As far as Takata was concerned, that is exactly what happened. After she had begged for help so sincerely, she heard a voice speak. The voice was loud and clear. "Today we call that clairaudience. I didn't know anything about that in 1935," explains Takata. "The voice said, 'Number one, get rid of all your illness. Just like that, you will find health, happiness and security.' I could not believe my ears until I heard the same message three times," reminisced Takata years later.

Within twenty-one days she was on a boat to Tokyo, hoping to find help there. Takata went to the Maeda Orthopedic Hospital in the district of Akasaka in Tokyo, the finest district in the heart of Tokyo, near the Royal Palace. The hospital was named after her friend, Dr. T. Maeda, whom she went to see. At that time, Takata's weight was down to 97 pounds. The doctor shook his head when he saw her. He said she would have to build up her strength before any thought of surgery could be considered. Takata and her two small daughters stayed at the hospital while she did.

After a few weeks, Takata was ready for surgery. While she was on the operating table, she heard the same voice speak again. It commanded, "Do not have the operation. It is not necessary." Takata pinched herself to be sure she was both conscious and sane. When she heard the voice speak the message three times, she quickly got down from the operating table and stood on the floor, causing great consternation among the nurses.

Dr. Maeda arrived, inquiring what all the commotion was about. Takata told him she was not afraid of dying during the operation, but wanted to know if any other form of treatment was available. He answered that there was indeed another form of treatment. "But it's a matter of time. How much time can you give it?" Takata answered, "If you can allow me, I would like that treatment." Dr. Maeda explained that she would have to work at it. "How much time have you got?" He insisted. Takata asked how long he thought it would take. Dr. Maeda replied, "A month, four months, maybe six months, maybe one year." "Because he said, 'maybe one year,' I doubled him and said, 'I can stay two years.'"

Dr. Maeda encouraged Takata to try the other treatment. He said, "What are we going on about? Two years is a long time. Go do the other treatment. If you don't respond to it, come back." He told the nurse to dress Takata and call his sister, Mrs. Shimura, who was the hospital dietician. Takata later learned that Mrs. Shimura some years earlier had been in a coma, dying of dysentery, when she was treated by the Reiki Master Chujiro Hayashi. After the treatment she came out of the coma and recovered.

Mrs. Shimura took Takata to Dr. Hayashi's offices where her introduction to Reiki began. As Takata told the story, "I was the last patient of the day. I didn't know what was going to happen. I was told to lie down. Two of Dr. Hayashi's practitioners worked on me. One on the eyes, head, sinus, thyroid; the other one worked on the rest of my body. Their hands were very hot. One of them said, 'Oh, these eyes are burning! Oh my! Terrible, terrible eyes!' I said, 'Yes.' The other was working with his hands on my body, in the number one position, he said, 'Oh, the gallbladder—buzzing, buzzing, buzzing.' See, and this is where the headache comes from.'

And when he went to the number two position he said, 'Oh, my goodness! Your pancreas—buzzing, buzzing, buzzing.' And so it went on. Number three position, number four."

"I can best describe what happened by citing the way it is referred to in the Bible, 'the laying on of hands.' I am a very curious woman. I said to myself, 'I am going to investigate how they are doing this. What makes me feel first the warmth, then actual heat emanating from their hands?' And I said to myself, 'Oh, I'm not going to argue now. Tomorrow I shall come alone and find out more."

The next day Takata arrived early. She wanted to be the first one to receive Reiki, so that way she could investigate where the heat was coming from. She looked under the table, at the ceiling, everywhere, but could find no cords or instruments. Then she thought, "Aha, they have a battery or motor hidden in their sleeves." Dr. Hayashi's assistants wore Japanese kimono with the long sleeves, which have pockets. They worked silently. Her moment came. As she was being treated Takata suddenly grabbed the practitioner at the sleeve pocket of his kimono. He was startled, but thinking she needed some tissue, he thoughtfully handed her some. Takata said, "No, I want to see the machine in your pocket." The practitioner burst out into uncontrolled laughter. He was sitting on a stool and almost fell down he was laughing so hard.

Dr. Hayashi, who was in the next room came in and said, "What is this happy, happy laughter? If there is anything funny, I want to join! Laughter is very good for you." The man said, "Oh, this lady from Hawaii says there are instruments here and she grabbed my pocket." Hayashi stood up and said, "That's not funny. This lady from Hawaii wanted to know how this thing works and all she could imagine was a battery." "Therefore," he said, "she was only expressing democracy. What she wants to know, what she wants to think, she spits it out. If she were a Japanese lady, she wouldn't open her mouth! 'What is it?' She'd go on all afternoon, brew her tea and as she nibbled her biscuit and sipped her tea, she'd still be thinking, 'what is it that makes the hand hot? What is it that makes the sickness, the pain go away?' And she would still be imagining, imagining, but not dare to ask any question. That's the difference of a Japanese lady, thinking not to display any emotion in public. But the Americans are very frank and they come right out with it. That is their expression, so there's nothing wrong about it."

Dr. Chujiro Hayashi (1878-1941)

Hayashi then turned to Takata and asked if there was radio in Hawaii. Yes, of course, she replied. He smiled and proceeded to give her his explanation of Universal Life

65

Force—Reiki. "All right" Hayashi continued, "This radio is a set (machine), not a radio station broadcast. If they (the radio station) broadcast speech, you get speech. If they are broadcasting music, you get music. See? And so what this little machine receives all depends on what the broadcasting station transmits. This is the same thing. In this great universe there is a great light, a great cosmic energy, the ether wave. In some countries they call this 'prana.' We know the secret, how to tap that and then tune into it. Then, you have the energy feeding you. That's how you get well. We can even do absent treatment when you go back to Hawaii, since I know your face very well. When you are sick again, I can contact you and send the energy right there."

In only four months Takata was cured of her complex problems by Reiki. She recognized that Reiki was her destiny and that she must bring it to the West. She begged to learn but they said no. "You are an alien," they explained. "This is born in Japan. Japan gave us judo, kendo, karate and all kinds of other arts, Ki and flower arrangement. But Reiki, no! That's only for Japanese."

Takata was not deterred in the least. Instead, she enlisted the help of her friend Dr. Maeda, who wrote her a strong letter of recommendation. The letter was then hand-delivered to Hayashi. Upon reviewing the letter, Hayashi felt compelled to call a special meeting of Reiki leaders where they agreed to allow Takata to become an honorary member of the group. She stayed on at Dr. Hayashi's healing center in Tokyo to study basic and advanced Reiki techniques for nearly two years. Before returning home to Hawaii, she learned from Dr. Hayashi what he called the Five Ideals of Reiki:

Just for today, do not anger
Just for today, do not worry
Just for today, count your blessings
Just for today, do an honest day's work
Just for today, be kind to all living things

Dr. Hayashi eventually visited Takata in Honolulu, Hawaii. He was deeply impressed with her and with her dedication to Reiki. Takata had been intensely involved in Reiki for three years. Hayashi acknowledged her gifts. Because of her zeal to learn, despite being both a foreigner and woman in a man's society, under Hayashi's tutelage she became the first Western Reiki Master. Her certificate reads as follows:

CERTIFICATE

THIS IS TO CERTIFY that *Mrs. Hawayo Takata*, an American Citizen born in the Territory of Hawaii, after a course of study and training in the Usui system of Reiki healing undertaken under my personal supervision during a visit to Japan in 1935 and subsequently, has passed all the tests and proved worthy and capable of administering the treatment and of conferring the power of Reiki on others.

Therefore, I Chujiro Hayashi, by virtue of my authority as a Master of the Usui Reiki system of drugless healing, do hereby confer upon Mrs. Hawayo Takata the full power and authority to practice the Reiki system and to impart to others the secret knowledge and the gift of healing under this system.

MRS. HAWAYO TAKATA, is hereby certified by me as a practitioner and Master of Dr. Usui's Reiki system of healing, at this time the only person in the United States authorized to confer similar powers on others and one of the thirteen fully qualified as a Master of the profession.

Signed by me this 21st day of February, 1938, in the city and county of Honolulu, territory of Hawaii,
(SIGNED) (Chujiro Hayashi)
Witness to his signature:
(Yoshio Hanao)
Territory of Hawaii
City and County of Honolulu

On this 21ˢᵗ day of February, A.D. 1938, before me personally appeared (DR.) CHUJIRO HAYASHI to me known to be the person described in and who executed the foregoing instrument and acknowledged that WHO executed the same as HIS free act and deed.

(W.Silva)

Notary Public, First Judicial Circuit, Territory of Hawaii

Hawayo Takata (1900-1980)

This was a high honor and Takata took it as such. She set out on a career that covered over 40 years of continuous Reiki practice and teaching. She succeeded brilliantly in her mission of bringing the seeds of Reiki to the West and planting them in many fertile souls.

First in dreams and later in waking meditations, Dr. Hayashi became aware in December 1940 that Japan would fight the United States and lose. As a retired naval officer, he knew he would be required to command a vessel and engage in the fight. He did not want to participate in the conflict.

As an enlightened human being, Hayashi knew the exact time of his death. Before passing, he called together the Reiki dignitaries and students in Japan. He also summoned Takata from the Hawaiian Islands. He designated her as the successor of his group. She was present as Hayashi left his body on May 10, 1941. According to Takata, the cause of death was a conscious, painless breaking of blood vessels.

Intending to return to Japan to further develop Reiki, Takata went back to Honolulu to put her affairs in order. However, before she could return to Japan, the Japanese bombed the United States at Pearl Harbor and war was underway. Many years passed. When Takata was finally able to return to Japan in the 1950's, she found the Reiki movement to be small and closed off. She spoke of this in classes she later taught in California.

Realizing that her role with Reiki was destined to take place outside Japan, Takata went home to the Hawaiian Islands. She practiced Reiki in Honolulu and gave classes at the University of Hawaii and elsewhere. She trained Japanese-Americans, native Hawaiians, and later, people of every faith and racial heritage.

She taught her students that Reiki is referred to in the ancient texts of Japanese Buddhism, sacred writings that go back many hundreds of years.

Takata was very clear that Reiki means Universal Life Energy and that it is not a religion. She explained it to her students this way: "Here is the great space which surrounds us—the Universe. There is endless and enormous energy. It is universal. Its ultimate source is the Creator. It can stem from the sun or moon or stars, but science cannot prove or tell us yet. But it is a limitless force. It is the source of energy that makes the plants grow and the birds fly. When a human being has pain or other health problems, he or she can draw from it. It is an ethereal source, a wave length of great power which can revitalize and restore harmony."

In the 1970's, Takata began traveling to the mainland United States to visit her daughter, Alice Furomoto, whose Japanese-American husband practiced general medicine in Iowa. Stopping in California, she began to give classes first to Japanese-Americans and then to people of other ethnic backgrounds. The first class in which people of other than Japanese origin participated was on Orcas Island, off the coast of Washington State. That was in 1973, the year John was working at Stanford Research Institute doing computer systems analysis.

John and his first wife, Beth Gray, met Takata on June 12, 1974, in two of the first Reiki classes held in the San Francisco Bay area. From 1974 to 1977, Takata gave numerous Reiki workshops at John and Beth's house. She was also a regular speaker at Trinity Metaphysical Center, where Beth was Pastor.

Takata told John that once she once had a studio in the Mojave Desert of California in the town of Twenty-nine Palms. Perhaps she got the money for this studio from heiress Doris Duke, the richest woman in the world at that time. Takata told John that Doris Duke took her on a round-the-world trip, during which Takata gave her regular Reiki treatments. They became close friends. The studio in Twenty-nine Palms was open for about a year, but Takata had to close it because it was too hot for her in the desert.

This pattern of visiting the US and teaching continued for Takata until late 1975 when she developed heart problems. She announced her retirement in 1976, but she never actually retired.

In late 1980 Takata suffered a final heart attack and died. A year after Takata's death, on the island of Hawaii, a week-long gathering of 17 of the 22 Reiki Masters trained by Takata took place. John was part of the gathering. He recollects, "We visited the temple where Takata's remains are kept, talked about Reiki and showed each other how we performed attunements. We acknowledged Phyllis Furomoto, Takata's granddaughter, as the new leader of the Reiki movement." This meeting set the stage for the 1983 formation of the Reiki Alliance, an organization of Reiki Masters who can trace their lineage back to Takata.

Phyllis had been studying with Takata for some time and had accompanied her on several workshops. Phyllis is a highly intelligent woman who speaks English with an Iowa twang but does not speak Japanese. Her main function as she sees it, is to be the cohesive center for Reiki as it has come to the West.

"One thing we did not think about at that early meeting in 1981 in Hawaii, and took quite a while before our omission occurred to us, was to establish criteria or make general provisions for the training and certification of Reiki Masters," says John. There is no standard procedure for the verification of a Master's credentials. Consequently, a great number of variations have developed from the original Reiki system being practiced and taught today. The Reiki Alliance is a stopgap measure. Only Masters who can trace their lineage from Takata are accepted for admission. The training for Reiki Mastership in the West, while quite specific, is an oral tradition. With an oral tradition, over time there usually are subtle changes in the original instructions. Western Reiki instruction is exceedingly vulnerable to such changes.

For example, in Reiki I, attunements are given during which trainees are conditioned into a shift in their energy blueprint. This shift makes it possible to give Reiki treatments without using one's own energy, to offer treatments without taking on a client's problems and to do self-treatments.)

You see, we all can deliver healing energy through our hands—it is part of our human heritage. Even if you receive altered attunements, you can still deliver hands-on energy, but the problem here is that you may be using your own energy and are likely to be tired after a treatment. Also, you usually cannot give energy to yourself and may be vulnerable to your clients' problems. Whenever we take calls from people who feel drained of energy after giving Reiki or who have picked up an emotional condition from their clients, it prompts John to recall his own introduction to healing in 1974, when a third of the "healers" at Trinity Center felt worse instead of better at the end of the 20-minute healing meditation (see chapter 1).

There is an even more serious and widespread problem. Since no universal certification procedure is in place, anyone can promote him or herself to be a Reiki master by declaration, without training. This situation has led to instant "masters" without any experience or seasoning attempting to pass the system on to newcomers, creating a multitude of misunderstandings and confusion about Reiki.

We prefer the term "Reiki" be reserved for The Usui System of Healing as passed down from Usui without alterations. We believe that Reiki should be taught as a system, just as it came to the West, as a knowable concept for both practitioners and recipients rather than a vast range of practices anyone chooses to do under the name of Reiki. Perhaps this will happen eventually. We know from experience the value of the specific Reiki practices. In the meantime promoting concern for each other and respect for individual differences will help us all move forward towards a world of harmony and peace. Reiki is circling the globe and that is

73

good, because Reiki has become a synonym for spiritual healing, another name for love energy.) We believe that having love and concern for each other is essential not only to survive the new millennium but in order to move to our highest potential as human beings.

Chapter 4
The Elements of Reiki

R eiki is a gift and an art, a simple, natural process for healing by the laying-on of hands. Every person has the ability to channel healing energy through his or her hands. It is part of our human heritage. In fact, laying-on of hands may be the oldest healing modality we have. Dating back many thousands of years, it appears near universally in cultures around the globe. (Rather than seeming unusual or phenomenal, healing by laying-on of hands should seem profoundly familiar, for it has been with the human community for millennia.)

Reiki is a part of this extensive history, since it is a particular approach that disciplines and refines a basic human ability. This chapter sets out our understanding of some basic Reiki concepts and principles. The following chapter details our specific approach to delivering a complete Reiki treatment.

Thanks to the sacrifice and research of Dr. Mikao Usui in recovering Reiki, we know that there are some advantages that distinguish it from other systems for healing by the laying-on of hands. These advantages make Reiki an ideal modality for anyone who is interested in healing the sick and comforting the afflicted.

However, only properly performed Reiki attunements provide these advantages, which greatly increase the flow of universal life energy (Reiki) through the practitioner while protecting him or her from absorbing or contracting the afflictions of the client. These properly performed attunements are the hallmark of Reiki.

Reiki harmonizes and normalizes body cells and processes. It is an actual force, a band of energy frequencies characterized by a gentle yet effective power. This power can revitalize and restore harmony to all people.

As defined by James L. Oschman, Ph.D., "healing energy—whether produced by a medical device or projected from the human body—is energy of a particular frequency or set of frequencies that stimulates the repair of one or more tissues." Oschman's book, *What is Healing Energy: the Scientific Basis of Energy Medicine*, documents how in recent years, scientists have been able to use a device called the SQUID (Superconducting Quantum Interference Device) to explore and measure the biological energy fields in humans and other organisms. The device shows that the healing touch characteristic of laying-on of hands pulses at a very low frequency, ranging from 0.3 Hz to 30 Hz. This range of frequencies appears to be an effective stimulant for tissue healing. Most of the signals emitted by healers fall in the range of 7-8 Hz. Reiki energy falls within this range.

A person offering a Reiki treatment serves, in a sense, as a semiconductor, transferring energy from a source to a subject. In the case of healing, the source is the infinite supply of universal life energy (Reiki), and the subject is the client. The process is biological rather than mechanical and is characterized by a bioelectric and biomagnetic energy flow. Interestingly, the flow of this energy is controlled not by the practitioner, but rather by the natural needs of the patient or client who is receiving the treatment. When people are in good health, they draw little energy in a Reiki treatment. When the need is great, the flow is very powerful and both practitioner and client will notice it.

In a manner of speaking, a Reiki practitioner cannot be said to heal as much as to deliver energy to the client, who then uses the extra energy to heal him or herself. The body is the healer. Reiki gives the body the strength to do what nature intends the body to do, normalize the functions. For example, if the pancreas is either not producing enough insulin or producing too much, Reiki will help to normalize insulin production.

Reiki practitioners need not have a medical background to use the technique and obtain good results. All we need to do is to deliver the energy and let the wisdom of the client's body utilize the energy as needed. For this reason Hawayo Takata developed a foundation pattern of hand placements and encouraged John to develop it further. If you follow the standard pattern when you are treating someone, you will directly cover his or her major glands, organs and energy centers.

Giving Reiki to another person actually increases a practitioner's vitality. Since the practitioner serves as a pipeline or channel for the energy flow, some of the energy is naturally assimilated by the practitioner; not the main force of it, but some of it. Energy flows only from the practitioner to the client, never backward. Thus, Reiki practitioners are protected from taking on a client's problems. This is an important consideration for all energy healers.

Attunements

Properly performed attunements (and we emphasize the word properly) are the hallmark of Reiki. Reiki differs from other healing methods in that a special formula is used by the

Reiki instructor to prepare trainees for the flow of healing energy and protect them from taking on the conditions of their clients. Only people who have received specific attunements from a properly trained Reiki Master can be considered true Reiki healers.

The attunements are a technical way of making a shift in a person's energy blueprint so that he or she can channel more energy through the chakras. Attunements constitute what might be thought of as a re-wiring of the human energy system so it can function in the service of health and healing. By the use of mantras, symbols, and movements, the Reiki Master is able to increase the chakras' energy flow while skillfully connecting or bypassing certain pathways called "nadis." These pathways serve to transport energy to different areas in the body much like acupuncture meridians do. This specific process results in the creation of a "true channel," for Reiki energy. Thus, anytime the hands of a Reiki practitioner touch "cells with a purpose," be it the self, another person, animal, or plant, healing energy starts flowing freely and strongly. It flows in through the Reiki practitioner's chakras following the new connections. It skips the practitioner's own energy system and enters into the cells of the recipient. This flow continues until the cells of the recipient fill up.

Properly attuned Reiki practitioners do not use their own energy in giving a Reiki session. They draw from the vast supply of life energy in the universe. Thus, they are not depleted of energy at the end of the session and so are able to treat as many people as they like. Further, they are not susceptible to picking up problems from their clients, a drawback of some other healing modalities.

Reiki Degrees

The original Reiki system as recovered by Mikao Usui has three levels or degrees, generally referred to as Reiki I,

Reiki II and Reiki III (also called Reiki Master). The training and attunements for each level are specific and explicit.
They were passed on with meticulous care by Chujiro Hayashi
and Hawayo Takata.

Reiki I—By the end of a Reiki I workshop, which typically occurs over either two days or four evenings, students
are able to channel basic Reiki energy for the healing of others, sense the energy as it flows and perceive areas of reduced vitality in order to better allocate their time during the
Reiki session. In addition, students are able to administer
Reiki healing energy to themselves. Reiki I involves four
attunements, the history of Reiki, a comprehensive review
of the patterns for hand placement, and practical experience.

Reiki II—Students who enter the second-degree Reiki
program typically have done much work with the tools provided for contact healing by the first-degree course. They
feel a commitment toward using those tools in service to others and wish to expand the knowledge and abilities they have
already acquired. At least three months have elapsed since
the first-degree course. No one has to tell them that Reiki
works. They have already had that experience.

Hawayo Takata used to say, "First degree, 20 horsepower;
Second degree, 100 horsepower—very powerful."

Participants in a Reiki II class receive another specific
series of attunements which opens them to additional energies. Students learn techniques for the expansion of Reiki
healing. The first technique increases the energy flow during the session. This procedure enhances and extends the
power and flow of Reiki energy through the hands. The second technique is used for treating clients with mental and
emotional issues. The emotional component of a disease may
be treated with this method (see Chapter 6.) Addiction, mental illness, depression and attitudinal problems can be addressed as well. Self-improvement and goal setting are also
facilitated with this technique.

566-GRAY

The third technique is a procedure for absent treatments, effective with anyone or anything from a foot to ten thousand or more miles away. We have worked with people over the years who have been able to feel when they are being sent an absent treatment. Likewise, the Reiki practitioner giving the absent treatment can feel the energy while it flows into the person receiving the treatment. Energy flowing into the chakras and the electromagnetic field, the aura, can also be felt. Absent treatments can also be used to address intellectual or emotional concepts. Thus, an emotional problem from a past situation may finally find closure. Future goals can be energized with Reiki and brought closer to physical reality. In a sense, there are no time or space barriers when it comes to Reiki healing.

Reiki III—The Master level in Reiki is the teaching level. This subject is covered in Chapter 8.

Cause and Effect

One of Hawayo Takata's guiding principles was to treat both cause and effect. While undergoing his Reiki Master training, John heard Takata say repeatedly that to heal with Reiki one must address cause and effect. If you can find the cause of the illness and remove it, then you will get rid of the effects. Takata trained her students to search for and attempt to eliminate the cause, rather than just focus on the symptoms. If the practitioner finds the cause and gets rid of it then the effects, or symptoms, dissipate. She repeated this over and over in her classes. If you treat only the afflicted area of the body, you may alleviate symptoms temporarily but permanent healing will not take place unless you treat the cause (see Chapter 6).

Takata believed that if a woman had problems with her eyes, she needed extra energy in the reproductive region. She often told the story of a young woman who became blind at age 13 for no apparent reason. Her mother took her to many physicians to determine the cause of blindness. None was found. When the blind girl was 17, her mother brought her to Takata for treatment.

Takata gave the young woman complete daily treatments for 28 days. On the 29th day, the young woman came in and said, "Mrs. Takata, you are wearing a pink dress and white shoes."

Takata was pleased and asked the young woman when she began to see. The woman replied, "Yesterday." Takata asked her whether anything else had happened yesterday. The young woman responded, "I started my first menstruation." Years later, Takata told John she had felt a substantial amount of energy drawn by the young woman's reproductive system. If she had treated only the eyes for blindness, she would have missed the real source of the problem, the reproductive system, and the young woman might never have regained her sight or initiated a healthy reproductive cycle.

Takata always encouraged complete and frequent Reiki treatments for long-lasting chronic problems, daily, if possible. She emphasized that if a health problem or illness has been around for three weeks or more, the whole body is involved in the healing process and therefore a full treatment is indicated.

Frequent treatments are just as important. Be consistent. Do not expect a long-standing condition to disappear overnight. Stay with it. Keep treating the condition and always offer a full treatment, so you can address the cause and not just the effects.

Reactions

Reactions may happen after a Reiki treatment in the form of a physical or emotional release in response to the inflow of healthy life energy. Waste products and toxins in afflicted bodily systems, organs or cells, are released and excreted from the body. Takata called reactions "bloodless surgery." Thus after a Reiki treatment or series of treatments, the client may develop a fever, discharge mucus, have a bout of diarrhea, or in some other way react to the infusion of healing energy by expelling or changing the energy patterns that have been causing disease or discomfort.

We have found that reactions occur for either or both of two principal reasons. The first is elimination of toxic substances. The Reiki treatment may be helping the person to expel toxins from the cells, but the toxins give a final kick as they leave the system. They may be released unpleasantly as a sore throat, a slight fever, a headache, or diarrhea. In such cases, up to three more Reiki treatments should be given, one each day for three days, to help the toxins flow out through the elimination systems of the body.

The second reason is that the person's system, or an organ within a system, may be unable to retain the Reiki energy. This happens typically when the person has had the problem for years, for example, a problem in the digestive system. After a long time, the system is so stressed and weak that it cannot make use of the energy and even seems to weaken further. Again, give the person at least three more complete treatments. The person will then be able to absorb and make a more effective use of the Reiki energy.

After experiencing a reaction, a client might think, "Oh, Reiki made me worse." When a person feels worse after a Reiki treatment, it usually means that the energy is taking effect and is beginning a process of internal cleansing.

Reactions can also be of an emotional nature. Sometimes emotional toxins, strong feelings that have never been processed, need to be released. These can take the form of extended crying or even laughing sessions. Lourdes gave a treatment once to a man with asthma. Afterwards, he said to her, "I don't understand why I feel so angry. You didn't do anything wrong, but this is how I feel." Cells hold memory of past emotions. Even if we no longer consciously recall the events, the emotions generated by them remain in cellular memory. Like peeling the layers of an onion, sadness, fear, anger and other disease-causing emotions can be released by Reiki energy in the form of emotional reactions.

Reiki will release only as much as can be tolerated by the client. Gently but powerfully, it will balance and harmonize the body, mind and emotions, helping create true health.

Practitioners need to understand what can happen following a Reiki session. A reaction usually happens after the practitioner has given a first session to a client and occasionally after the second time. The sequence is quite predictable. Therefore, it is important to recognize that sometimes toxins from the body are released, particularly the first one or two times the client experiences Reiki. They may be released in an unpleasant way through a sore throat, a slight fever, headache or diarrhea.

We suggest that the client visualize the toxins flowing out through the breath, perspiration, urine and feces. This visualization will contribute to the elimination cycle. We also suggest the client drink plenty of water as well, to facilitate the passing of toxins.

After a reaction, the client should rebuild. A modification in diet, the addition of exercise to the daily routine, meditation or some other health change may be indicated. If the condition is chronic, the rebuilding and re-establishment of health may take some time. If the condition has been around for only a short time, then the treatments will be effective more swiftly.

Back in the early 1980's John gave a workshop in Yakima, Washington. About a year before the workshop, a woman named Doris had received a clean bill of health after intestinal cancer. She had been told that she was in remission, which was confirmed through monthly checkups. She felt wonderful.

One month before the workshop, Doris found that a lump had formed in one of her breasts. The lump was malignant. She was only given only a few months to live. She took the chemotherapy treatments the doctors recommended.

Wondering how else she could help herself, Doris decided to sign up for a Reiki class. This particular class was being given on four evenings, Tuesday through Friday, instead of over a weekend. Having learned about Doris from his sponsor, John chose her the first night of the class for a demonstration on how to give a Reiki treatment.

The next morning John got a call from the workshop sponsor. The sponsor said that Doris had called, describing terrible intestinal pains she had felt during the night. She said that she could not finish the workshop, but instead was going to the doctor and probably the hospital. John identified this situation as a classic example of a reaction. He called Doris and said, "If you don't finish the rest of the workshop, you'll regret it for the rest of your very short life!" She heard the message, thought it over, and came to the class that evening.

The second night John demonstrated on Doris again. He also shared information with the class about physicians who conducted a study in the 1950's noting an event-related commonality around cancer. The physicians found that typically, from six to twelve months before the onset of cancer, an event occurred that caused the cancer patient to adopt an attitude of helplessness and hopelessness. Such an event might be the loss of a job, a divorce, a child getting into trouble, or some event of equally serious emotional consequence. The kinds of event that can cause an attitude of helplessness and hopelessness vary from person to person. The physicians concluded that helplessness and hopelessness apparently can communicate themselves to the cells in the immune system so that they stop working. This allows malignant cells to begin forming a tumor and soon after, the cancer starts developing.

The average healthy human being produces at least 300 cancer cells a day. Our immune system finds these cells, gobbles them up and we are fine. However, when our immune system malfunctions, it is unable to do its job. We start developing more of these cells than the system can destroy. They start clumping together and growing. Soon there is a cancer. This scenario is not limited to just cancer, or to diseases affected by weak immunity. Many other parts of the body can be profoundly influenced by feelings of helplessness or hopelessness. A variety of maladies can develop.

John told the class that there are many different ways of looking at the past. Every person holds perhaps a few dozen internal snapshots of both comfortable and uncomfortable events from their life. Individuals can review their lives from the viewpoint of either all the sad things or all the wonderful things that have happened to them. We can choose what to hold close and ponder on. John explains, "We have a choice of what to look at. For example, we can dwell on the time at the altar when she never showed. Or the time it was rainy and cold at the beach and the sandwiches got soggy. Or, instead we can choose to remember joyful events. We can control which snapshots to look at!" John continues, "We can focus on remembering comfortable events, such as, the graduation dance where we danced until dawn and had a magical time. Or the day we went to the beach and the sun and sea breezes felt sweet and sensuous. We might remember the relaxing sound of the surf rolling up on the beach. We have a choice, with both the big and the little things in life."

It takes courage and persistence to put your attention towards pleasant things but it can be done. That second night at the workshop, Doris heard this discussion loud and clear, for it had been her pattern to choose to remember the bad, difficult and annoying things in life and to dwell morbidly upon them.

During the third class session, John again demonstrated Reiki on Doris. She shared with the class that she felt better. By the fourth night, she told the class, "I'm feeling better than I have in months."

John stayed in Yakima over the weekend and gave Doris a private session. The next week he got a letter from the workshop sponsor. Doris had gone to her physician for a regular chemotherapy treatment during the week. While there she persuaded them to give her a scan. She was free of cancer.

"My comment to Doris that if she didn't come to the rest of the workshop, she would regret it for the rest of her very short life, was apparently helpful," John recalls. "She came back to class and she got well. If I had not been forceful in my request for her to come back and stick with the workshop, she might be dead now."

The point of this story is that in a sense, Reiki practitioners are not really healers. We simply deliver energy. Practitioners do not have the responsibility for the way Reiki energy is taken and used by a client. The real healer is the person receiving the energy. How they take that energy and use it is their responsibility.

By all means be careful not to predispose the client for a reaction with what you say before or during a treatment. If a client has a reaction, interpret it as a sign that Reiki is working. You then have the responsibility of giving that person another two or three sessions. Continue with complete Reiki treatments and work to eliminate the cause. The effects will then dissipate in due course.

Animals and Plants

With Reiki you can energize any cell or organism, even water. Give Reiki to animals just as you would to humans. Work in patterns covering the major sections of the body so that glands, organs and energy centers all receive attention. Lourdes Reiki's our dog, Oscar, one side of the body at a time. Animals are much more perceptive of energy than we are. They have auras and chakras too. Some animals, such as cats, are super-sensitive to energy flow and become restless during long Reiki treatments, so keep their sessions frequent and short. Fish can be treated too, right in their aquarium. Just place your hands against the outside of the bowl or tank. Reiki will pass through glass. The fish will respond to the goodness of the energy and come to the hands. Absent treatments work best for treating animals you do not know well or in those in the wild. You do not want to risk a bite!

For plants, hold the pot and gradually energize the earth. Systematically work your way up the trunk, branches and leaves. Plants respond quickly. "Reiki" water acts as plant fertilizer. "Reiki" a container of plain water for five to ten minutes before watering.

Self-Treatment

Another advantage of Reiki is that you can treat yourself as well as others. Both uses are simple, straightforward and effective. After giving a treatment, you feel better than before because you are not using your own energy reserves. Just the opposite happens. The moment you touch yourself, another person, animal, plant or anything that has cells with a purpose, Reiki will start coming in through your chakras and flowing to your palms and fingertips. As the Reiki energy flows out your hands and into the cells of the body underneath, the cells recognize the life-giving energy and draw on it. Much like a weak battery, depleted cells require more time and energy to recharge. Cells control the degree of energy draw. The more depleted they are, the stronger the flow. Reiki flow is automatic, controlled entirely by the cells of the recipient. There is no need for special preparation or mental concentration on the part of the practitioner. Takata called it "automatic concentration."

(Automatic concentration and not utilizing your own energy reserves are two of the features that make Reiki different from other energy healing systems.) Other systems, such as Qi Gong and Therapeutic Touch, require the practitioner to draw from his or her own energy reserves, thereby limiting the number of possible treatments and perhaps creating certain risks if the practitioner is not in good health.

John practices the following the self-healing routine. "At night I do my head and my neck, my eyes, the side of my head that has to do with hearing and my throat. If I have had a particularly emotional day or if I wake up and can't go back to sleep, I place my hands behind my head. I usually do that at night. Then I do my torso in the morning. If I've had a big meal, I do my abdomen to help digest it. When I get a sore throat, which happens infrequently, I'll do five or six hours on my sinuses, throat and chest. Occasionally I treat my liver. I treat any position as little or as much as I want to, since I know where my health challenges are. Reiki self-treatment is an effective stress-reduction method. I am a much more peaceful person now than when I was in the business world. I am much healthier than I would have been if I had not learned and practiced Reiki. I've outlived the average age for men in my family and expect to continue living longer and in good health."

Often, people become deeply relaxed while giving self-treatment and they often doze off, which is fine. Enjoy the nap. You can do Reiki when you are asleep, when watching TV, while driving or even while sitting in a reception area waiting for the dentist or a business appointment. Just rest your hands wherever you need the healing energy and it will flow, quietly and unobtrusively, even while you are napping.

Lourdes prefers doing the treatment all at once, usually in the evening at bedtime. "While lying on my back in bed or on a couch, I place my hands over my eyes and forehead. If my arms get tired, I put a pillow under my elbows. I stay three to five minutes in each position. Then I do the sides and back of my head. I work my way down the front of the body from the throat to the bottom of the torso, covering the neck, breasts, heart, lungs, diaphragm, digestive system, intestines, female reproductive system and bladder. I also treat my adrenal glands, kidneys, ureters, sacrum and coccyx by reaching around the back for a more direct effect. If you cannot reach your back, treat from the front of the torso and stay longer to allow the energy to penetrate. I finish with the back of my knees and the soles of my feet. The Insomnia Point, an extra point known in Japanese acupuncture, is located in the center of the heel. Treat the back of the head and the Insomnia Point if you have a difficult time falling asleep.

"I began doing Reiki on myself right after I received the first degree. I gained many physical and emotional benefits, including an improved immune response and stress relief. My eyesight got better after six months of self-treatment. Takata's recipe for eyesight improvement is to treat positions one, two and three of the second pattern ten minutes each on a daily basis in addition to the standard self-treatment routine. She also recommended eye-strengthening exercises before the sessions. 'Follow this routine for a minimum of three months before you can expect results,' she told her students."

Problems that generally do not respond to allopathic medicine may improve with Reiki. After several years of consistent self-treatment, two students, each with lifelong thyroid deficiencies, were able to discontinue thyroid medication with their physicians' approval. Several female students with fertility problems were able to conceive after practicing Reiki for some time. The last one we trained sent us a letter two months ago announcing the birth of her twins.

Rheumatoid arthritis, hypertension, allergies, pre-menstrual syndrome and other chronic illnesses can often be improved by self-treatment, keeping in mind that conditions present for years are unlikely to disappear overnight. Consistency is the key.

Reiki self-treatment can serve as preventive maintenance. It keeps cells energized, making it more difficult for disease to set in. If you decide to do Reiki daily for at least six months, you should notice a significant improvement in your emotional and physical health. We hope you discover, just as we did, that Reiki self-treatment gives beneficial results.

Going Mainstream

Reiki is known for its effectiveness in inducing the relaxation response through physical touch without body manipulation. Reiki helps patients slip into a deep state of relaxation, relieving tension and anxiety. It enhances the abilities of the immune system to fight bacteria and viruses and stimulates the brain's production of endorphins, a hormone that decreases the perception of pain.

Over the years Reiki has gradually proved itself in mainstream medical settings. Numerous hospitals and clinics across the world have instituted complementary therapeutic programs so that patients can receive Reiki treatments. Many nursing and therapeutic massage associations have approved Reiki for continuing education credits. This trend of bringing Reiki to the mainstream healing centers of our culture is likely to continue, since it has proven to be an effective complement to the scientific treatments of allopathic medicine.

A Gift

Taking a Reiki class could be one of the very best gifts you have ever given yourself, not only for the promotion and maintenance of your own health. The added gift is being able to help and comfort the people you love.

Chapter 5
The Usui-Gray
Integrated Reiki
Treatment

The Usui-Gray Integrated Reiki System® has evolved over 25 years. It includes six steps, all of which are outlined in detail in this chapter. We believe it is important to understand where the treatment system came from and how it has evolved.

After recovering Reiki through his intensive studies and his long fast on Mount Kurayama, Mikao Usui developed the Reiki system of treatment through the early 1920s. He died in 1926, passing on the tradition directly to several masters, including Chujiro Hayashi. Hayashi then held the system for 15 or 16 years, making his transition in 1941.

The Reiki system that Hayashi employed is similar to the system that Mikao Usui used. It is based on the Oriental understanding of healing that has long recognized the human energy field. Hand placements are related, in a general way, to key meridians and acupuncture points. Hayashi's concept of Reiki healing was a complicated one: for example, treating the ears alone involved eleven positions specific to that area. It undoubtedly took quite a while to learn the system.

In 1941 Dr. Hayashi gave Hawayo Takata the manuscript

presented in Appendix A. It was his instruction manual on how to do Reiki, organized by specific ailments.

As readers will discover, Dr. Hayashi's manual has a high degree of complexity and redundancy. The same positions are repeated over and over again for many of the ailments, with slight variations and optional positions. His system was, and still is, effective. However, it is also cumbersome.

Takata learned and practiced the Usui-Hayashi system, but at some point realized that Hayashi's list of treatments would be repetitive and confusing for Western students. Over time, with mounting experience and study, she made a discovery. She found that if she channeled energy with a series of hand placements covering key points in certain patterns on the body, it worked as well as the complex approach Hayashi had documented. Takata combined many of the hand positions found in Dr. Hayashi's manual, standardizing the patterns so that every Reiki treatment would be the same. In this way she created what she called a "foundation treatment," making the system much easier to learn. This was her genius and one of her major contributions to Reiki.

Takata's foundation treatment focused on the torso and the head. Four basic hand positions were for the torso, three positions for the head, and no positions over the heart or on the back. She supplemented her foundation treatment with optional positions, depending on the nature of the client's problem and where it was physically located. "Go to the problem," she would say.

For her foundation treatment, Takata began with the area of the torso, covering the liver and gall bladder, then moving on to the stomach, pancreas, spleen, transverse colon, small intestine, reproductive system, ascending and descending colon, and bladder. This first sequence took a total of four placements of both hands. She had three hand positions for the head, also treating the back of the head in some cases. In her time, this simple procedure was a complete foundation Reiki treatment.

Takata worked with this Reiki system as a practitioner day in and day out for 40 years before she started teaching it to Westerners. She developed a substantial amount of experience using it and discerning what worked and what didn't work. She knew how to convey it to a non-oriental class so that it was easy to understand, easy to learn, was sufficiently comprehensive, and could be taught over the course of three or four evenings.

For her clients, Takata also did a hand manipulation along the spine to improve blood circulation. We do not teach it because it involves manipulation of tissue by running fingers on either side of the spine all the way down from the neck to the tail bone (coccyx). In many jurisdictions, this requires a massage license. Instead, we teach a pattern on the back, legs and feet which accomplishes the same result without tissue manipulation.

So, Reiki evolved from something complex to something clear and simple, something anyone, even a child, could learn quickly and easily. On many occasions while John was her student, Takata said, "I have simplified the system." She typically taught her Reiki I class in three or four evening sessions.

Later, building directly on Takata's work, and under her supervision, John developed the specific procedures and patterns of the Usui-Gray Integrated Treatment presented in this chapter. In the Usui-Gray Reiki Integrated Reiki System®, more basic positions were added, including the heart, eight positions on the back, and four on the head and face.

The Usui-Gray system developed gradually in the late 1970s as Reiki was taking root in America. After Takata had instructed many people through her classes in California, the Trinity Metaphysical Center in Redwood City, California became the early focal point for Reiki in the US. There were regular Reiki sessions each week before the services. Several massage tables were set up with two or three Reiki practitioners stationed at each table delivering energy to all who came in need of healing. Often as many as 20 people received treatments before the service. In addition to John Harvey Gray and Beth Gray, dozens of people were Reiki channels and participated. Eventually the group began to add other hand positions so that more practitioners would have an opportunity to give Reiki at the same time. Many of the previously optional positions became standard.

For example, Takata worked on the heart as an optional position. John intuitively felt that there was a need for energy over the heart and thymus gland to balance that area, so he added this hand position to the standard Reiki treatment.

John also added positions for the back, the kidneys and adrenal glands, the spinal nerves that energize all the organs in the body, and a large area of musculature that, in many people, is greatly stressed. John found that by applying Reiki in these standard patterns, one could better energize and balance the whole person.

In time, he added positions for the knees and feet, recognizing the need to supply energy to the lower body and feet to balance, energize and ground them. As many people know through Reflexology, nerves and reflexes on the feet correspond to all glands and organs. Treating the feet is an effective way to treat reflex points for the whole body.

Some of the practices of the Usui-Gray Integrated Reiki System® were developed with aid of the Hemi-Sync® techniques based on what John learned from his extensive studies with Bob Monroe and the Monroe Institute in Virginia. These techniques can be very useful tools. Eventually John became a Hemi-Sync® instructor. Hemispheric Synchronization is a system in which music is used to produce two separate beats with a differential. For example, 100 Hertz is directed in one ear and 110 Hertz in the other ear. The brain recognizes a differential of ten Hertz, and that is what the brain hears. When this happens, the two hemispheres of the brain synchronize and harmonize. They vibrate the same. This creates a state of super-relaxation or super-learning, a technology that has been quite successful dealing with anxiety, depression, pain and many other conditions. It helped John to gain many important intuitions into the effective application of Reiki.

Over time, through his study and healing work, John kept refining and adding to the standard procedure for giving a Reiki treatment until it developed into six steps and a set of clearly defined hand positions in three distinct patterns. Takata was present while all of this was developing. She knew John was adding procedures and positions. She agreed with it, participated in it and encouraged it. This is how Takata's original foundation treatment evolved into the Usui-Gray Integrated Reiki System®.

John's process was to take Takata's system and, via his own intuitive insights, try variations and carefully observe what happened. By 1980, the year Takata passed into Spirit, the Usui-Gray Integrated System® was complete.

The six specific steps of the Usui-Gray Integrated Reiki System® treatment are set out in the latter part of this chapter. Following are some general principles for giving a complete Reiki treatment.

Giving a Treatment

The body is the healer. Reiki gives the body the strength to do what nature intends the body to do; normalize the functions. In offering a treatment, several important elements for practitioners must be kept in mind.

Ideally, the client is lying on the table on his or her back. If possible, you should use a folding massage or bodywork table because they can be adjusted to a comfortable height for you as you stand with your hands resting on the client for an hour or more. It is important that both the client and the practitioner be comfortable and in a stress-free posture. In a pinch, a sturdy kitchen table can be used, or even a door set upon sawhorses or some other stable support. If you use the latter, you will want some foam cut to size or several thick blankets to cover the table, so the client will not be resting on a hard wooden surface.

Takata would give treatments sitting cross-legged on the floor. Most people are not so agile or flexible and would soon find this position uncomfortable. Beds are generally a bad idea, for they are too low; the practitioner has to bend and twist during the session, and can stress his or her back. You can, however, give a good treatment to someone sitting in a chair.

We strongly recommend that if at all possible, you work on a bodywork table with a clean sheet for each new client. If you are serious about Reiki, this is a worthwhile investment. Make sure the table is at a comfortable height for you and can be adjusted so that you are not bending and straining your back. Some practitioners complain of back pain after the treatment. This can easily be avoided by keeping your back straight, your hands in front of your body, legs slightly bent at the knees and thighs gently resting against the bodywork table. Keep your hand pressure light. Pressing down hard does not improve the energy flow. It does just the opposite.

During a Reiki treatment, energy is transferred through three patterns of hand placement. The first pattern covers the front of the torso. The second pattern is applied to the head and neck. The third pattern covers the back.

The energy transfer of a Reiki treatment vitalizes body cells. By the end of the treatment all body systems (blood supply, nerves, organs, etc.) are operating in a stronger, more balanced and normal way. Delivery of the energy is standardized. The Reiki practitioner does not need know anatomical or medical details.

Our job as Reiki practitioners is to deliver energy. The client will take what he or she needs. We do not diagnose and we do not prescribe. We simply deliver energy.

Focused intention to heal is always helpful on the part of the practitioner, but not essential. In Reiki, the energy flows automatically without concentration, prayer, or meditation. You can be driving or working at your desk and do Reiki. You can be asleep and Reiki will still flow. It is a simple system to use when you are ill. Once a person is properly attuned, the energy will flow automatically.

Except for emergencies, always begin the Reiki treatment with your hands on the front of the body, placed on the upper left side of the client's abdomen, over the stomach, pancreas and spleen.

Place your hands in the first position of the first pattern. The cells beneath your hands will recognize the energy and then start to receive. The practitioner will, in most cases, feel the draw of energy begin and build. When the cells under the hands have received all the Reiki they need, the practitioner will sense a subtle slowdown and decline in the flow of the energy, although sometimes that sensation may increase again, as Reiki flows in an undulating manner, like a sine curve.

At the time of the first drop-off in the flow, the practitioner should move one hand slowly and gently into the second position of the first pattern. When a connection with Reiki energy is felt in the new location, then the second hand is gently moved and positioned beside the first. This is done to keep a continuous flow of energy throughout the session, rather than the stop-and-go sensation that would occur if the practitioner took his or her hands completely away from the client. The continuous flow helps the client to remain in a state of deep relaxation. If you move your hands too fast, you will break contact with the client's energy field and the client may experience a slightly unpleasant or jarring sensation.

Hold your hands lightly in each position until you feel the energy flow begin to diminish. The client's cells will take only as much energy as they require. At that time, the practitioner will feel the energy flow begin to slow down. You will know that it is time to move on to the next hand position. Move your hands one at a time, slowly and carefully, never abruptly, to the next position.

When you are doing Reiki, the cells underneath your hands will receive energy directly from your hands. The more depleted that part of the body, the stronger will be the flow. If, when doing Reiki, you feel a strong flow, it is because that area is depleted. Stay there until those cells fill up and you perceive that flow has slowed down. You will have a subtle but definite feeling that the flow has slowed or stopped. You know then that it is time to move on to the next position. Sometimes it is hard for new Reiki practitioners to measure this, which is why we recommend you stay two to three minutes per hand position. After a while, you will feel the energy rise as you settle into a new hand position, and then fall as the cells beneath the hand become charged. You will no longer need to time yourself. If necessary, you can stay longer in any position where there is a problem or injury. Another of Takata's axioms was, "No such thing as a Reiki overdose."

If time is limited, you need to be able to get to all the positions. It is a good idea to set aside, an hour or an hour and a half for a session as beginners. With practice, you will have a better perception of what the flow is. You will be able to feel a difference, which may be a tingling, shaking, heat, or pulsating.

It is important to not try to control the energy. Let it flow and trust the wisdom of the energy and the wisdom of the client's body. The person receiving the Reiki treatment will take what they need at the rate they can best receive it. The practitioner does not need to do anything more than become of a quiet mind and deliver the energy. Trust the wisdom of nature to do what it needs to do. This aspect of Reiki healing cannot really be taught in a class. It must be learned through experience.

During the session, your reference point will be the median plane of the body, an imaginary line running from head to foot, which divides the body into left and right halves. Depending on which side of the table you are working, you will either place your fingertips or the heels of your hands on this median plane.

If you are uncomfortable or tense, you can impede upon the energy flow. A good analogy is to imagine water coming out of a garden hose. If you bend or twist the hose, the water will slow or stop flowing. That is exactly what happens when we press down too hard or become tense while delivering Reiki energy. In addition, you will also be non-verbally communicating stress and tension to your client.

Keep a clock near you the first few months of practice to make sure you move every few minutes, except in cases where your clients have told you that they have a problem. In that instance, you may want to stay five to seven minutes over the afflicted area. You cannot overload a cell with Reiki energy. Takata liked to tell a story about a man who was dying of cancer. She trained his wife and teenaged children to give him Reiki. They gave him Reiki 24 hours a day, taking shifts. Someone was always with him. He went into remission. The greatest benefit comes from giving a full Reiki session if the problem has existed longer than three weeks. This is why we recommend you to budget your time.

Polarity is not important in Reiki. It matters not what side of the table you work from, nor does it matter whether your client's head faces north, east, south, or west.

Likewise, it makes no difference what type of clothing

the client is wearing. Reiki penetrates all materials; metal belt buckles, artificial and natural fibers or plaster casts. A client does not need to remove any clothing or supportive equipment. Reiki will work right through all fabrics and materials, reaching in to illuminate and recharge the energy field of the client.

People who have been practicing Reiki for several years, perhaps five years or more, seem to have much stronger and more even chakras than people who have been practicing Reiki briefly. This suggests to us that whenever a Reiki practitioner is delivering Reiki, and the energy starts flowing through his or her chakras supplying the energy for the treatment, the chakras function as valves allowing an extra supply of ki to flow through to the client. We do not use our own energy in Reiki. This is a major distinction from some healing systems where the practitioner is drawing on his or her own energy resources and can do no more than two or three sessions in a day before being exhausted. Reiki practitioners can deliver as many treatments as they choose.

The Six Steps of A Complete Reiki Treatment

Step 1. Counseling

Begin in a relaxed and patient manner. Take your time. Don't jump into a session. It is important to talk with the client before the session, to discuss their general health, health history and any specific problems.

Ask your client what is going on. Ask them what their problems are. Remember that unless you are licensed to do so, Reiki practitioners are not allowed to diagnose nor prescribe, but we can use our intelligence and intuition to help. We need to ask clients as much about their physical problems as possible. It is also appropriate to ask about emotional difficulties, for example, if there is any discomfort at work or at home. You may ask whether they have a clear direction in their life or whether they feel lost. Allow them to talk about their concerns. Listen carefully. Try to understand the person and to extend your professional compassion.

Whenever we do a counseling session with a client who has a physical problem, we always ask, "When did this first start? What was going on in your life at that time? What underlying attitude did you have toward what was going on?" We ask this because frequently six months to a year before the onset of a difficulty, an event happens which creates an attitude of helplessness and hopelessness in the self. This can communicate itself to the body and manifest physically (see Chapter 6). Helping the client discover their event and how to shift their awareness is the start of resolving the illness.

Always obtain permission to touch before starting the hands-on session. Clients, especially those who have suffered physical or sexual abuse in the past, need to know they are safe during the treatment. If they indicate they are uneasy with your hands on their physical body in certain positions, ask if you may place your hands three to four inches above that position instead. Tell all your clients that they have full control of the session and may end it whenever they wish.

When we do initial counseling before a Reiki session, we like to make a contract with our clients that we will not get into a discussion afterwards in an attempt to analyze the session. Instead, we plan to talk on the phone the next day, and arrange for a time to do so. We have two reasons for the follow-up phone discussion. We want our client to leave in a peaceful and restful state. Intellectualizing the session right after completing it defeats that goal. We do, however, want honest feedback about the treatment to learn whether the client experiences a reaction (see Chapter 4).

If the client does experience a reaction, you need to get

the client back to follow-up with two or three more treatments as close together as possible, over the next three days if that can be arranged. If you cannot do this, try to arrange for the person to meet with another Reiki practitioner. We have a lengthy list of qualified practitioners in the United States, and can serve as a resource for this in many cases. It is important to do these follow-up treatments in order to help the body cleanse and detoxify, or to revitalize a system if it has dropped energy or become depleted.

During the Reiki treatment, it is possible that the client will gain insight into emotional difficulties or perhaps sense a road they should be taking to deal with important life situations. If this kind of insight doesn't arise during the session, it might happen during the night after the session.

Many practitioners find it helpful to take notes before and after the treatment and keep these on file in order to follow the client's progress.

Step 2. Scanning

We teach a four-step process for scanning. Have the client lie face up on the bodywork table. If the room is cool, you may cover the person with a blanket. It will not interfere with your scan of their energy system or the Reiki treatment.

1. *Sensitize your hands.* Hold both hands in front of you, fingers spread slightly apart, palms facing each other. Slowly move your hands together and then apart several times. Gradually you will begin to feel a field of energy being created between the sub-chakras located on the palms of your hands. This may feel like pressure, heat, tingling energy or your own individual perception. To many people it feels like a ball of energy. If you are having difficulty, try rubbing the palms of your hands together for a moment to build up a bit of friction. Once you feel the energy, your hands are sensitized. They are now in a feeling mode and you are ready to scan the aura. This action is not necessary to deliver Reiki,

but it is an aid to scanning. Any time that you have difficulty feeling a chakra, you may want to sensitize your hands again and go back to re-scan it.

2. *Feel for general physical vitality by checking the outer edge of the client's aura.* Standing close to the bodywork table, raise both your hands in the air as high as you can, palms facing down over your client's chest around the breastbone area. Your thumbs should be about one inch apart. Slowly bring your hands down towards the client until you feel the same sensation you felt while sensitizing your hands. This sensation, in this position, represents the edge of your client's aura.

Stay within the chest area. It is the most accurate place to measure the physical aura. Take a few moments and feel the edge of the aura. The farther the edge is from the physical body, the stronger is the vitality of your client. The closer it is to the physical body, the weaker the client's vitality. The measurement of general physical vitality is a fairly dependable tool for determining the frequency and duration of Reiki treatments. If you feel that the client's general physical vitality is high, perhaps 20 or more inches from the physical body, it is likely that the Reiki treatment will be relatively brief, perhaps 45 minutes to an hour. If, on the other hand, you do not feel the edge of the aura until you are within a few inches of the client's body, you can suspect that the person is severely depleted of energy and will need longer and more frequent sessions to recover.

Lourdes once worked on a man with Hepatitis B. He was frail and weak, spending most of his time lying on a mattress on his living room floor. His liver was so damaged by the disease, he was on a waiting list for a liver transplant. Lourdes performed the customary scanning before offering Reiki. She was astonished to discover that the man's physical aura was only two inches from his body. She knew right away that he lacked the vitality to fight the viral infection on his own and would need extra help. Lourdes attuned the man to Reiki I and taught him the self-treatment, suggesting that he perform it as frequently as possible. She returned once a week to give him a treatment herself.

Since a Reiki self-treatment is effortless, the man was able to follow the advice. He did not need to summon his own energy to do it. Lying on his mattress for hours each day, he placed his hands in the various Reiki positions. As the series of treatments progressed, the man's general vitality improved and the height of the aura increased. He no longer needed to spend all day resting on the mattress. He began to get busy around the house and returned to work part-time. A month and a half after the Reiki treatments commenced, his physician was amazed to see his blood test come back negative for Hepatitis B, the only patient the doctor had ever known to have the test come back negative after having been positive without having any other allopathic treatment.

3. *Scan the Chakras.* Notice which of your hands was more sensitive and felt the aura most strongly. Then drop the other hand by your side and prepare to scan the chakras, using the more sensitive hand. Sometimes people discover that their dominant hand is the most sensitive. Sometimes it is the other way around. Some people do not notice a difference in the sensitivity of their hands, in which case they may use whichever hand they prefer. Regardless of which hand you use, you may wish to practice scanning the chakras with your other hand in order to develop both hands equally.

Scan each individual chakra to determine its strength, particularly between the root and the throat. When you notice that one chakra is weaker than the others, you may suspect that the band of glands and organs around that chakra may be vulnerable to problems.

If a chakra is weak, that part of the body may not be receiving the energy it needs. Our understanding is that the chakras serve as entry points for energy. Their job is to supply the cells of the body with additional energy beyond that

105

which the body takes from food and oxygen. If one chakra is not as open as the others, you can suspect that the glands and organs being fed by that chakra are not getting enough energy from the outside and may be vulnerable to problems. Chakra deficiencies are discussed in detail in Chapter 6.

Scan each of the seven main chakras and also the sub-chakras located on the knees and the soles of the feet. Place your hand, fingers spread open, palm down, facing the client's body over the general vicinity of each chakra. Hold your hands two to three inches in the air above the client's body. Gently pass them back and forth through the general area of the chakra. Perform this scanning motion a few times over each chakra until you are able to feel and assess its flow. What you will feel is a cylinder of energy about an inch or an inch-and-a-half in diameter. Start with the crown chakra located on the top of the head.

Next, move to the brow chakra above the middle of the forehead, right between the eyes. Move to the throat chakra at the base of the neck. Next, scan the heart chakra, located in the middle of the chest between the nipples. Now move down to the solar plexus chakra located at the V between the ribs. Then scan the lower abdominal chakra located about an inch below the navel. Next, slant your hand at a 45-degree angle to feel the root chakra, since it comes in at an angle to the perineum, between the anus and the genitals. Find the knee sub-chakras located on the front of the knees, and the foot chakras under the arch of each foot.

The chakras that seem to affect the physical body most are the throat, heart, solar plexus, lower abdominal and root. The crown and brow chakras do not seem to impact physical health as directly, but instead seem to have purposes related to spiritual development.

4. *Look for "zings."* Zing is a word John uses to describe what appears to be a static electric break in the aura. These breaks in the bio-electric field, or L-field, as described in the

work of Harold Saxon Burr are discussed in Chapter 6. To
the hands and fingers of a Reiki practitioner, zings feel like
weak static electricity shocks. They seem to be located directly over the area of the body where a problem exists.
To find zings, comb your hand through the aura steadily
and smoothly, from the head toward the feet, just as you might
comb your fingers through a pool of water. Feel with your
fingertips for slight disturbances in the overall flow and
smoothness of the aura. These are zings. When you detect a
zing, you may or may not know precisely what part of the
body or organ it corresponds to, but you will know that there
is a disruption in the aura. Ask your client if anything is going
on in that area or has gone on in the past. If the zing is strong
and the client is unaware of it, you may wish to suggest that
they get it checked.

A zing can represent one of three things: a present problem, a past problem that has healed and left an "energy scar"
in the aura, or a developing problem that has not yet manifested physically. Oriental medicine teaches us that disease
first manifests itself in the energy body before the pathology
can be detected. It is easiest to treat with Reiki in its early
stages. This way, we can help maximize the body's healing
potential and increase its chances of eliminating illness. The
Chinese philosopher Lao Tzu said, "Even the biggest problem in the world could have been solved when it was small."

In conclusion, we have come to understand that all the
components of the human energy system are important and
merit the attention of Reiki practitioners. The root chakra is
just as important for the supply of its energy as is the crown
chakra. Reiki can help bring all the aspects of the energy
anatomy into balance and that can translate into fuller physical and emotional health.

It is often said that you can't learn to ride a bicycle by
reading a book. Likewise, scanning requires actual experi-

ence and practice, but once the skill is grasped, it is a natural and effortless process.

After completing the four steps of scanning, you may wish to discuss your perceptions with your client, or to make notes. Then you are ready to proceed with the Reiki treatment itself.

Step 3. Opening Spiral

The opening spiral is a procedure developed by Brugh Joy, M.D., and adapted by John to Reiki (see Chapter 6). The opening spiral begins by placing your hand over the client's heart chakra, moving clockwise, and pausing at each chakra to deliver energy into it. This jump-starts the energy-delivery cycle and helps the client utilize more Reiki for healing purposes.

Start an opening spiral with one hand hovering just over the client's heart chakra. Relax and wait in that position for 5 to 15 seconds, until you feel you have a connection with the energy of that chakra. Then move your hand clockwise, one chakra at a time, in a spiral pattern as indicated in Illustration 1.

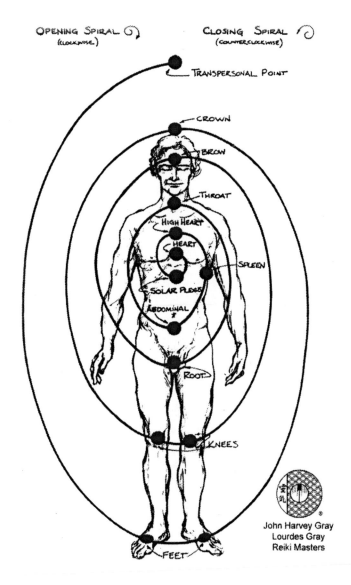

Illustration 1—The Opening Spiral.
The Reiki practitioner begins with his or her hand over the heart,
and proceeds in a clockwise manner from energy center to energy
center.

109

From the heart chakra move to the solar plexus chakra, and again pause until you feel good contact. Continue in this manner to the high heart (a sub-chakra), the spleen (a sub-chakra), lower abdomen, throat, root, brow, knees (do both at once using both hands), crown, feet (do both at once using both hands), ending with the transpersonal point. The transpersonal point is several inches above the crown where the energy of the aura turns and falls like an egg-shaped fountain around the body. To feel the energy of this point hold the back of the hand toward the top of the head and pull the palm side outward. Move your hand away from the head until you feel the transpersonal point. The sensation tends to be quite noticeable. Some systems consider the transpersonal point to be the eight chakra.

Toward the end of the treatment, the fifth step, the Reiki practitioner will perform the closing spiral, reversing this procedure, starting with the transpersonal point and moving counter-clockwise from chakra to chakra and ending at the heart.

Step 4. *The Three Patterns*

During a Reiki treatment, energy is transferred in three patterns. The first pattern covers the front of the torso; the second pattern is applied to the head and neck; the third pattern covers the back of the torso, the back of the knees and the soles of the feet.

Delivery of Reiki energy is standardized within the Usui-Gray Integrated System®. The Reiki practitioner does not need to know anatomical details, but in many situations it will be helpful to have a basic understanding of the human body and how it functions. We have included information describing the glands, organs, nerves and tissues that underlie, and are thus affected by, each of the hand positions.

First Pattern: Front Torso

Except for emergencies, always start a Reiki treatment on the front of the body, on the client's left upper abdominal quadrant. Have your client lie down on his or her back, or sit, if for some reason they are unable to lie down.

Imagine that the client's body is divided into two equal halves, left and right, by a median line running lengthwise from the head to the feet.

111

The Reiki Positions
1st Pattern

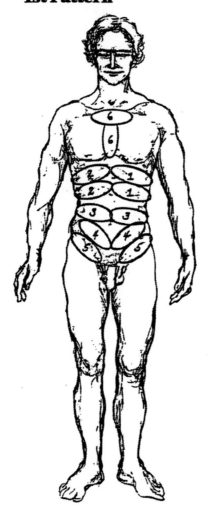

John Harvey Gray
Lourdes Gray
Reiki Masters

Illustration 2—The First Pattern.
The numbered ovals show the correct hand positions on the front
of the client's torso.

Hand Position 1:
Feel for the end of the sternum or breastbone, the xiphoid process. Place your hands below the breastbone, on what is known as the left epigastric/hypochondrial region. Hypochondrial comes from the Latin root "hypo" for under and "chondrium" for cartilage or ribcage, so, the word actually means "under the ribcage." Either your fingertips or the heels of your hands should be on the median line, depending on which side of the client's body you are working from. Notice that men have longer breastbones than women, so you might have to adjust your hand positions accordingly. Your fingers should be gently closed. Your hands should be side by side, parallel to each other forming a pair of "heat pads." In this position, your hands are over the stomach, spleen, part of the pancreas and part of the liver. By starting the Reiki treatment with the digestive system, the treatment will help any food in need of processing to move along. It will also dissipate tension held by the diaphragm. This helps the client relax and become more open to the benefits of the energy flow throughout the treatment.

Takata said that the digestive system is the general motor of the body. If you can get it to working right then you can get everything else to work right as well. Digestion starts in the mouth where food mixes with saliva and its digestive enzymes. The partially digested food then travels down the esophagus into the stomach where it mixes with hydrochloric acid and other enzymes to form a semi-solid mixture called "chyme." The chyme is moved by the muscle action of the stomach walls, called peristalsis, into the duodenum, or the mouth of the small intestine. In the small intestine, the digestion of food is completed and nutrients are absorbed.

The stomach is located in the upper middle and left part of the abdominal cavity just under the diaphragm. The lower part of the stomach, the pylorus, is the narrow part of the

113

stomach that joins the duodenum, the first part of the small intestine.

Lateral to the stomach on its right side is the spleen, the largest lymphoid organ in the body. It can contain up to a pint of blood. The major functions of the spleen include filtering and destroying bacteria and other foreign substances, destroying old red blood cells, storing iron and serving as a reservoir for blood. Because the spleen contains white blood cells, which kill bacteria, it is key to the immune system. Therefore, from this very first position the practitioner not only is helping to energize and harmonize the digestive system but also the immunological system.

The first position also affects the pancreas. The pancreas is a gland about six to nine inches long resembling a fish in its shape. The "head" is located in the C-curve of the duodenum, the "body" sits behind the stomach, and the "tail" touches the spleen. The pancreas is both an exocrine gland (secreting into a duct) and an endocrine gland (secreting into blood or tissue). The exocrine tissues secrete digestive enzymes that travel to the small intestine and help break down our food. The endocrine tissue is located in the pancreatic islands, which are embedded in the exocrine units of the pancreas. Two kinds of cells, alpha and beta, make up the islands. The alpha cells secrete glucagon which increases blood glucose levels, and the beta cells secrete insulin which decreases blood sugar levels.

Some Reiki programs advocate starting a treatment with the head. We have found that most of our clients consider this starting point too invasive and so do not benefit as much as they could from the session. It is best for clients to be fully relaxed by the time the practitioner is working in this area, so we always begin in Position 1 of the first pattern.

To review: the first hand position affects the digestive process, including the structure and function of the stomach, the pancreas, parts of the small intestine and liver, and affects the immune system through the spleen.

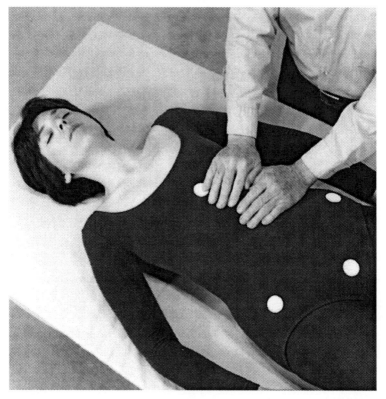

Pattern 1, Hand Position 1.

Hand Position 2:

When you are ready to move to the second position, lift up one hand very softly and slowly, then place the hand gently on the right side of the client's body. When you feel the energy flow begin, you may gently lift the second hand and set it down beside the other hand on the right epigastric/ hypochondriac region. When moving your hands, never move rapidly or slide them. You are not doing massage. Abrupt movements can be jolting to the person receiving energy.

115

In the second hand position, you are working on the liver, the gall bladder and the right tip of the pancreas.

The liver is the largest gland in the body, weighing about three to five pounds. It is located just under the right side of the diaphragm. The liver has four major functions: detoxification, bile secretion, metabolism of proteins, fats and carbohydrates and storage of some vitamins and minerals. Chemicals from our foods, toxins from the environment and from medications gather in the liver. They stay in the liver where, through a series of chemical reactions, they are converted to a solution that can pass through the kidneys and out of the body. If the practitioner is working on someone who is receiving chemotherapy or radiation, it is important to give energy to the liver to help detoxification.

The liver secretes bile, which is a strong alkaline. Bile salts aid the body in absorption of fats. They also help to eliminate breakdown products of red blood cells. Bile is stored in the gall bladder, a small sac-like organ. The gall bladder is located on the undersurface of the liver. While bile is being stored in the gall bladder, it becomes concentrated. Later when digestion occurs in the stomach, the gall bladder ejects bile into the duodenum of the small intestine to aid in digestion of fats.

In summary, with the second hand position Reiki assists the digestive and metabolic processes and aids in detoxification. Hydrochloric acid breaks down food so it can pass to the small intestine. The gall bladder sends bile that helps to break down fats. The final stage of digestion in the small intestine is a process that separates the waste material that passes to the large intestine from the nutrients that pass through the wall of the small intestine and go on to nourish the body. The nutrients go from the small intestine to the portal vein that carries them through the liver. The liver cleanses those nutrients so the body can safely use them. The liver is also able to manufacture vitamins and store sugar for release when it is needed.

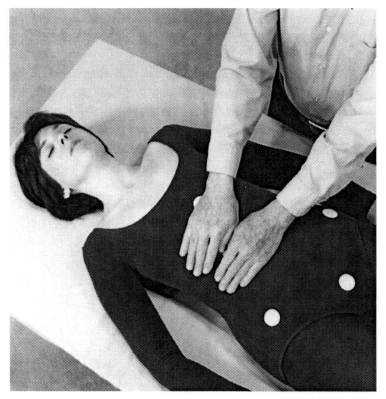

Pattern 1, Hand Position 2.

Hand Position 3:

Hand position 3 is just below positions one and two. The hands are placed in line, one in front of the other, at the waist; one hand should be on the left side and one on the right side, with some overlap. It does not matter which hand is left or right.

In Position 3, your hands are over part of the small intestine and the transverse colon of the large intestine.

The large intestine is divided into three segments: the

cecum, the colon, and the rectum. The colon is further divided into four sections: the ascending colon, lying vertically on the right; the transverse colon, passing horizontally at the waist; the descending colon, lying vertically on the left side; and the sigmoid colon, coursing downward toward the rectum in an S-shape.

The large intestine absorbs water and electrolytes from the digested food that passes through it. Voluntary and involuntary muscle contractions move the contents along toward the rectum. Once the food is absorbed through the 20-plus feet of small intestine, the waste material is pushed along through the large intestine. In position 3, you are treating the transverse colon and small intestine.

If you are working with a child or small person, positions 1 and 2 will cover the area that normally make up positions 1, 2, and 3. Thus, you can proceed from Position 2 directly to Position 4.

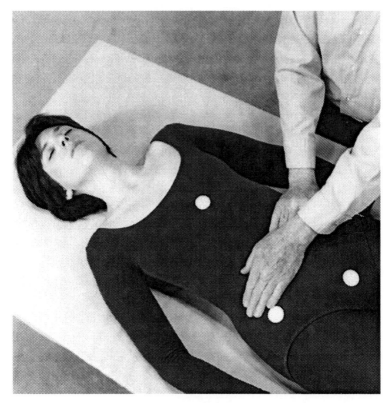

Pattern 1, Hand Position 3.

Hand Position 4:

This position is a little tricky at first, because your hands need to form a "V" within the abdominal cavity inside the pelvic bones. To do so, place the hand connected to the arm that is closest to your client's head on the near side of the "V" with your fingers pointing to the opposite foot. Your other hand will be opposite, forming the other side of the "V," with fingers pointing to the opposite shoulder. The "V" hand placement is done for the comfort of the practitioner, not because of polarity. As mentioned before, polarity is not a factor in Reiki.

Position 4 is a real key for healing. Whenever there is

something wrong in the body, this position draws a lot of energy. The organs and glands located under the hands in position 4 include parts of the large and small intestines, the urinary bladder and the ureters and the organs and glands of the reproductive system.

The ascending and descending colon is also located under the hands of the practitioner. The small intestine is under the palms and fingers of the hands as they overlap. The small intestine meets the large intestine at the ileo-cecal valve in the lower right quadrant near the pelvic rim. The ileo-cecal valve (the ileum is the end of small intestine, the cecum is the beginning of large intestine) is a sphincter muscle, which controls the flow of digested food from the small to the large intestine. Sometimes the flow becomes blocked or reversed. Reiki to this area can assist the healthy functioning of the valve. The appendix is also located in this quadrant.

The urinary bladder, which stores and then expels urine, is found just behind the pubic bone. Urine is produced in the kidneys, which are located at the back of the body on either side of the spine at the base of the ribs. Urine then travels to the bladder by way of the ureters, extending from the kidneys to the posterior surface of the bladder.

The reproductive organs and glands that are under the practitioner's hands in Position 4 include the male's prostate and Cowper's glands and the female's uterus, ovaries, fallopian tubes, and vagina. Other parts of the reproductive system including the male gonads, genital ducts, and external genitalia are not treated from this position. If they specifically need to be treated, then go directly to that area.

The male prostate is a donut-shaped gland lying just below the bladder. The urethra passes through the "hole of the donut." A great many older men, especially above age 50, have enlarged prostate glands, which squeeze the urethra, causing difficulties with urination. Reiki can help.

The female uterus is a pear-shaped organ located between

the bladder in front and the rectum behind. The uterus functions in three processes: menstruation, pregnancy, and labor. The ovaries are the female gonads. Their functions are ovulation and hormone production. They are located one on each side of the uterus, below and behind the uterine or fallopian tubes. The uterine tubes extend from the uterus toward the ovaries. The outer end of each tube curves over the top of each ovary and opens into the abdominal cavity.

After ovulation, the discharged egg enters the abdominal cavity and finds its way to the fallopian tube. Fertilization of the ovum normally takes place in this tube before it travels to the uterus to implant itself for the duration of the pregnancy. If fertilization does not occur, the uterus sheds its lining.

The vagina is a distensible tube located in the pelvic cavity below the uterus and between the bladder and the rectum. Its functions include receiving seminal fluid from the male, serving as the lower birth canal and excreting uterine secretions and menstrual flow.

Hawayo Takata said that if a woman had a problem elsewhere in the body, it would often be reflected in the need for a large amount of energy at this hand position.

This is a wonderful hand position for treating a pregnant woman. Many midwives use it. When there is a risk in the pregnancy, this position may help the mother carry the baby to full term. Reiki is also helpful when a person has a hard time conceiving, since it helps to energize the glands and organs.

To summarize: Position 4 is important for healing of the entire body. You are not only treating the digestive organs and reproductive organs and glands, but because of the wide-reaching effects of both the digestive system and the hormones secreted by the glands under your hands, you may also be affecting conditions in other areas of the body.

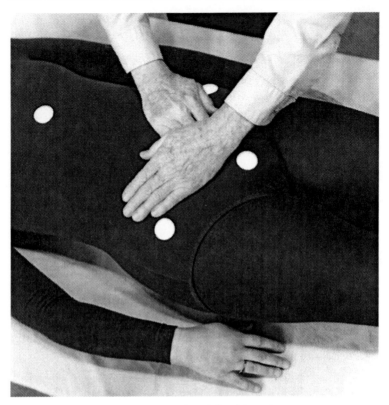

Pattern 1, Hand Position 4.

Hand Position 5:

Move slowly and carefully, one hand at a time, from Position 4 to 5. The hands should rest below the pelvic bones, right on the hip joints. Use the same hand angles as in position 4. If you have difficulty finding the proper position, ask your client permission to raise the leg and then place your hand where the crease is at the juncture of the leg and the pelvis. We call this position "the hinges." Remember to be sensitive of a man's anatomy in this position.

The major blood, nerve and lymph vessels pass through this area, as well as major acupuncture meridians to and from the lower limbs. Lymphatic fluid from the legs and external genitals drains through clusters of inguinal lymph nodes, which are located here. Lymphocytes, monocytes, non-granular white blood cells and plasma cells are formed here. Bacteria, cancer cells, and other harmful micro-organisms that flow into the nodes are phagocytosed (engulfed and swallowed) by specialized white blood cells called reticuloendothelial cells. Thus, Reiki energy in this position also helps the movement of lymph and helps reduce excess fluid in bodily tissues.

Giving Reiki in this position not only helps the immune system but also helps to move energy down to the legs. Any time the immune system is involved in fighting an infection, even if the client is pre-symptomatic, there will be a strong draw of energy here. We have found that we can often predict whether a client will come down with a cold or flu by the amount of energy being drawn in this position combined with a low "general physical vitality reading" while scanning.

In cases of malignant tumors, be sure to give plenty of energy to lymph nodes, as the cancer cells often break away from the tumor mass and enter the lymph nodes to create new growths.

Because this is the "hinge," or the hip joint, where the thigh bone meets the pelvis, hip joint movement problems should naturally be addressed by treatment here.

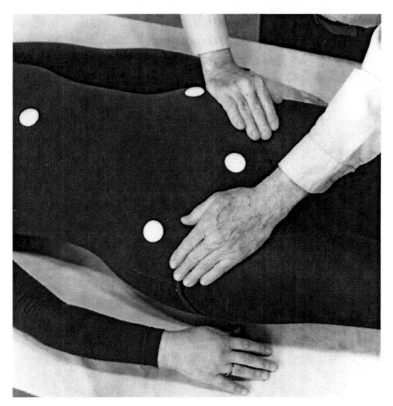

Pattern 1, Hand Position 5.

Hand Position 6:

If your client is a woman, your lower hand (the one that is farthest away from the client's head) should be placed on the breast bone with the other hand across the top, forming a "T" just below the clavicle. For a man, your hands may be parallel. In position 6 the hands are over the heart, lungs, and thymus gland.

The thymus gland is the central organ of the lymphatic system. It is located in the mediastinum, the middle section of the thorax between the two lungs. It is posterior to the sternum or breast bone, and anterior and superior to the heart. It extends up into the neck as far as the lower edge of the thyroid and below as far down as the costal cartilage of the fourth rib. The thymus serves as the source of lymphocytes-specific T-cells. After maturing, the T-cells leave the thymus to circulate to the lymph nodes, liver and spleen. After birth, the thymus also secretes a hormone that enables lymphocytes to develop into plasma cells, which synthesize antibodies. These protect the body from foreign proteins.

The heart, which is essentially a muscular pumping device, is located in the mediastinum behind the sternum, between the second and sixth ribs and slightly to the left of midline. It sits between the two lungs. The lungs extend from the diaphragm to a point slightly above the clavicles and against the ribs from front to back. The function of the lungs is to distribute air to the aveoli where gas exchange occurs.

For a woman, the breasts, also located in this region of the body, are the mammary glands. Their function is to secrete milk for the nourishment of infant children. Occasionally blockages occur in milk ducts causing mastitis or inflammation, or milk may not flow for some other reason. In this case a woman may seek Reiki treatment for the healthy functioning of lactation. In addition, many women seek Reiki treatment for breast cancer or other benign breast lumps.

If a female client is having breast problems, ask for permission to treat. If the answer is yes, take a sweater, pillow or towel and place it on the area to be treated as a barrier for modesty. First, place the barrier on the breast, then place your hands on the barrier and treat. The barrier will not interfere with the energy flow and will allow it to penetrate fully. The energy will flow through whatever is used with no problem. If the breasts are treated, also treat the lymph nodes under the arms (see optional position for treating the axillary lymph nodes and sides of ribs). Reiki will help whatever is going on there to just pass through.

In summary, in Position 6 you are affecting the immune function as well as the major organs of the circulatory and respiratory systems.

125

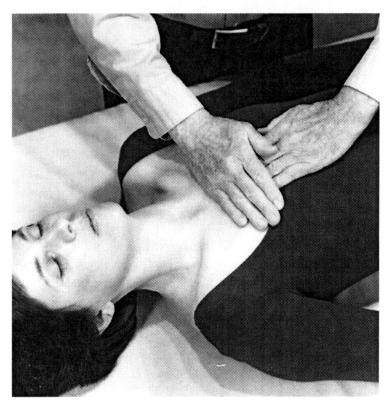

Pattern 1, Hand Position 6.

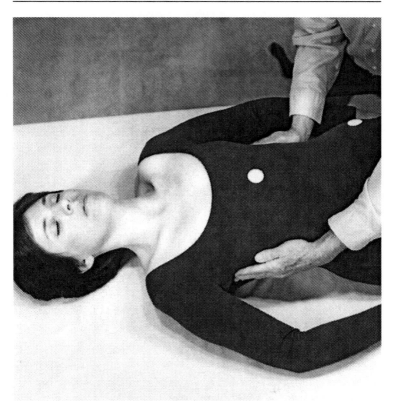

Pattern 1. Optional Position for the axillary lymph nodes and sides of ribs.

Second Pattern: Head and Neck

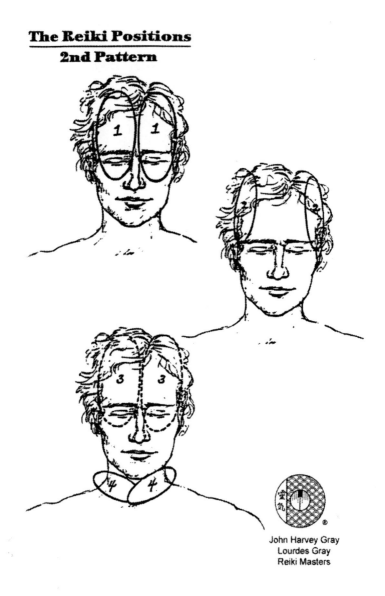

Illustration 3—The Second Pattern.
The numbered ovals show the correct hand positions on the head.

Hand Position 1:
Place a tissue over the client's eyes for cleanliness. Then lightly place your hands over the eyes. Your fingertips should line up with the lower edge of the nostrils, with thumbs next to each other. Position 1 affects the eye, eye muscles, nerves, frontal sinus, nasal cavity, brain, pituitary gland, and pineal gland.

The pituitary is a dual gland, which lies buried deep within the cranial cavity. It is often referred to as the "master gland" because it secretes hormones, which exert control over the structure and function of the thyroid, adrenals, ovaries and corpus luteum.

The pineal is a small cone-shaped gland that lies near the third ventricle of the brain. This gland is sometimes called the "third eye" because it is located near the center of the forehead and is influenced by the amount of light entering the eyes. It secretes the hormone melatonin. Its function appears to control cycles such as sleep and menstruation. In the days before electric light, the pineal gland regulated a woman's menstrual cycle in accord with various natural cycles of light. The modern convenience of electric light may be impacting these cycles. This is seen with hens, whose pineal glands are located on the top of the head. Chicken houses always have the lights on because the pineal gland, reacting to light, tells the chicken when to lay eggs. The steady light forces the chicken to keep laying eggs. One wonders what the impact of electric light has today upon the rhythm of women's menstrual cycles.

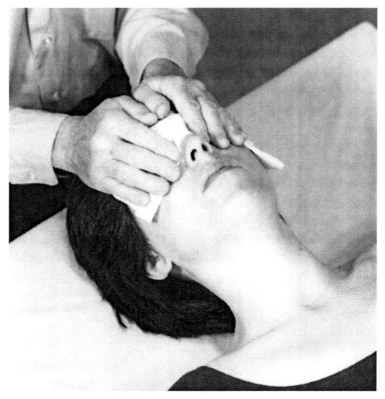

Pattern 2, Hand Position 1.

Hand Position 2:

Place the hands on the temporal lobes of the head, in front of the ears. Notice that the ear is not covered. The fingertips line up with the lower end of the ear.

In Position 2, the middle and inner ears are under your hands; you are affecting hearing and also balance, which is controlled by the inner ear. Use this position for inner or outer ear infections. This is also a good position for treating morning sickness in a woman who is pregnant. You are still giving energy to the brain and to the pituitary and pineal glands in this position. And you are still working on eye related issues.

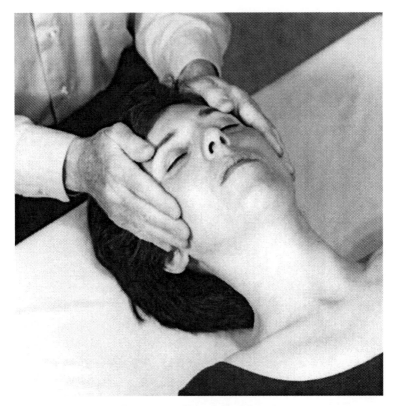

Pattern 2, Hand Position 2.

Hand Position 3:

To begin Position 3, tip the head gently to one side and put one hand under it. Scooping your fingers under the head, place your hand so that your fingertips are just under the base of the skull. Bring the head back to center balancing it on the hand. Place your other hand beside it, cradling the head with both hands at the base of the skull. Hold the head with fingers held tightly together.

Reiki to Position 3 affects the visual cortex, the part of the brain that interprets what the eyes see as sight. It also affects the brain stem. The brain stem contains ancient basic functions like hunger, thirst, the heart beat, temperature control and mood swings. If you are working on a client with emotional difficulties, this position treats that specific condition. Likewise, if you are working on a child who is irritable, this position will help with the crankiness. If the client is having problems falling asleep, treat this area. You can also use this position in a self-treatment and you will fall asleep quickly.

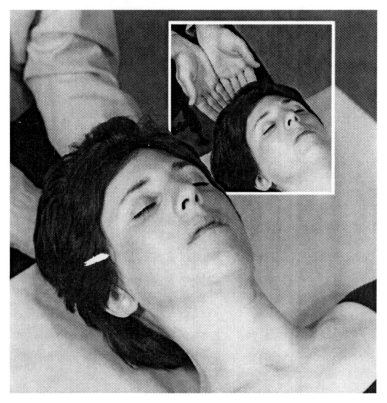

Pattern 2, Hand Position 3.

Hand Position 4:

To move to Position 4, open your palms one hand at a time. Rest your elbows on the table to keep arms relaxed. With your hands, create a platform parallel to the floor, making a bridge over the neck. Rest your hands on the chin or chest. Do not touch the throat.

This position will give energy to all the tissues of the neck, the larynx, trachea, salivary glands and the thyroid and parathyroid glands, which have an important regulating effect on the metabolic rate and calcium balance.

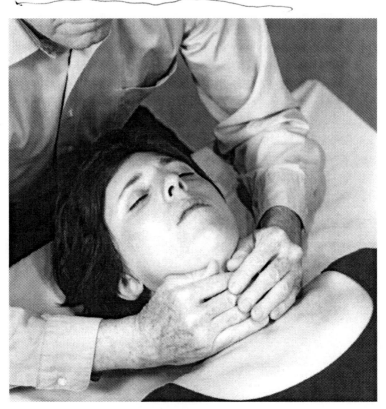

Pattern 2, Hand Position 4.

133

Optional Positions
Ear and Side of Neck

Cover the ears and sides of the client's neck with one hand on each side of the head. This position gives energy to the ears and is effective for ear infections.

Importantly, this hand position also gives energy to the carotid artery on both sides of the head and neck. The carotid artery brings blood to the brain. It has chemicals that control blood pressure. Reiki will help to normalize either high or low blood pressure. This is a specific position for blood pressure and for people who have a tendency for, or who have had, strokes. The carotid artery can become clogged with plaque. Reiki energy helps to break down the plaque. If you are holding this position and notice that the carotid artery feels hard, be sure to treat it. Takata taught to stay here also if the carotid artery feels soft and mushy.

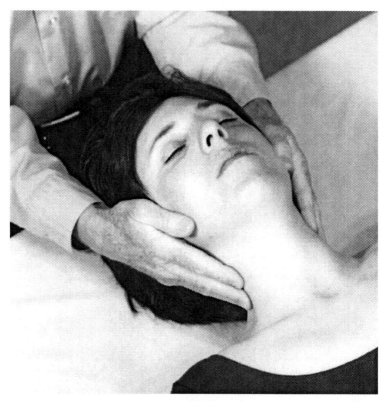

Pattern 2, Optional hand position on ears and the side of the neck.

Head Set

The "headset" is another optional position. Place the heels of your hands together bringing them over the top of the client's head, so that they are resting over the crown from one ear to another. Here, you are energizing the part of the brain that contains the motor muscle neurons. Reiki in this position helps the brain communicate with muscles. Use this position for Lou Gehrig's disease, MS, Parkinson's disease, cerebral palsy and stroke.

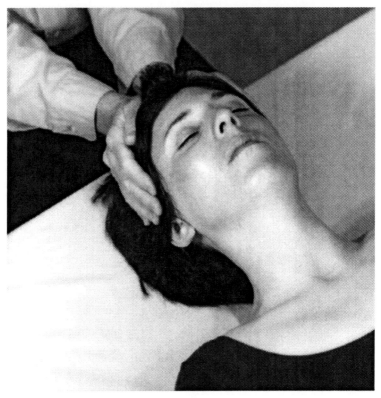

Pattern 2, Optional hand position over the head.

Lips, teeth, gums and tongue

To treat any of these problems, place tissue over the mouth and erect a platform with your hands. Make sure not to place the hands directly on the mouth.

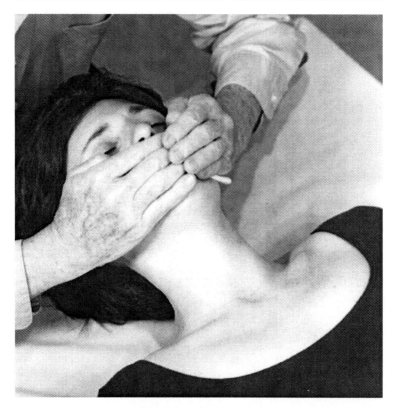

Pattern 2, Optional hand position for lips, teeth, gums and tongue.

Pattern 3: The Back, Legs, and Feet

This is a long pattern and is divided into three parts, moving from the shoulders to the waistline, from the waistline to the end of the torso, then to the legs and feet. It doesn't matter which side you start on, as long as you use the spine as a midline. Depending on which side of the client you are standing beside, and the position you are using, touch either your fingertips or the heels of your hands to the spine.

The Reiki Positions
3rd Pattern

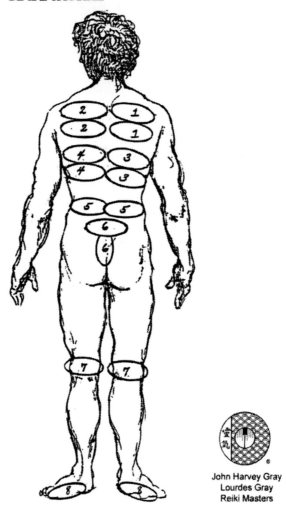

John Harvey Gray
Lourdes Gray
Reiki Masters

Illustration 4—The Third Pattern.
The numbered ovals show the correct hand positions on the back.

Hand Positions 1 and 2:

Start on either side placing both hands in position one, using the spine as the midline. The two hands are placed lightly side by side. In the first two positions, you are treating the back of the heart, lungs, back of the breasts and thymus gland.

In 1976, Takata had John give her Reiki privately on these two positions. What John was actually doing was treating her heart, but he did not know that at the time. Takata had suffered a heart attack in 1975 but kept it a secret from everybody.

Note: If the client's spine is extra-sensitive, place your hands one to two inches above the body and treat from there instead.

139

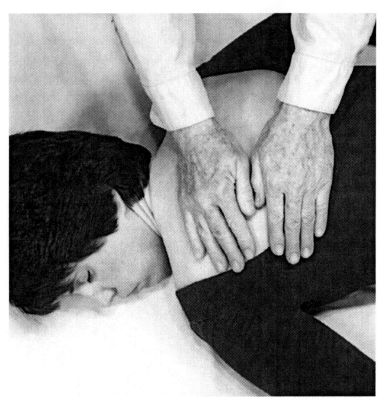

Pattern 3, Hand Position 1.

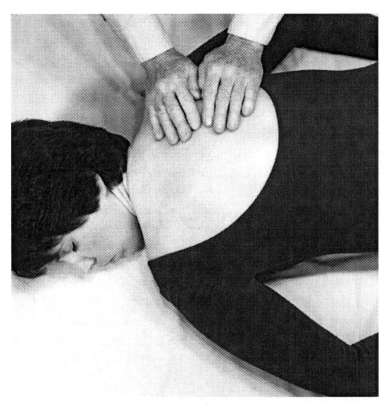

Pattern 3, Hand Positions 2.

Hand Positions 3 and 4:

Move your hands, slowly and gently, to the positions just below 1 and 2, so that you are working your way down the back from side to side. Adjust the number of positions to the size of the client. For instance, a tall person requires many more positions than an infant would. The idea is to cover the whole broad area of the back.

In positions 3 and 4 you are on the back of the stomach, part of the pancreas and the spleen. On the right side, you are on the back of the liver and the gall bladder.

Remember, our bodies are packed like suitcases. Thus, in these positions you are not only working on the digestion, but also on the kidneys and adrenal glands. Kidneys are the major filters of the body. They filter 60 gallons of blood every day and help to balance our acid and alkaline levels. The kidneys remove toxins from the body, uric acid out of the food we eat and waste products from the body. Working on the kidneys helps them to do their job better and pass along any substances that might start building up and forming pebbles. There are many examples of kidney stones passing harmlessly during Reiki treatments. It is best to treat this problem early on, when the kidney stones are small.

The adrenal glands provide us adrenaline, the "get-up-and-go" hormone, which gives us the strength to take care of ourselves during an emergency. When human beings lived in the forests and jungles, adrenaline gave us the strength to pick up a club or run for our lives when danger appeared on the scene. Today, because of the ongoing stress in the lives of many people, the adrenals often secrete too much.

When you are working on people who have had an emergency situation or who are under a lot of stress, be sure to treat the adrenal glands. If you can't treat them from the back, do them from the front (positions 1 and 2 of the first pattern).

Many tall persons require extra positions to cover the back to the waist. Add positions as necessary.

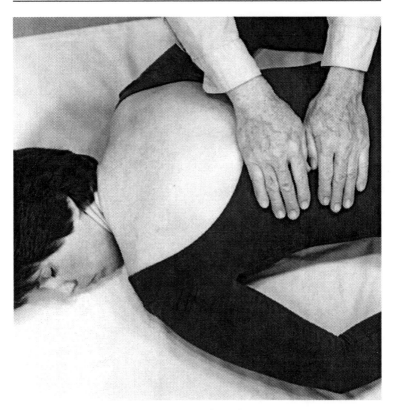

Pattern 3, Hand Position 3.

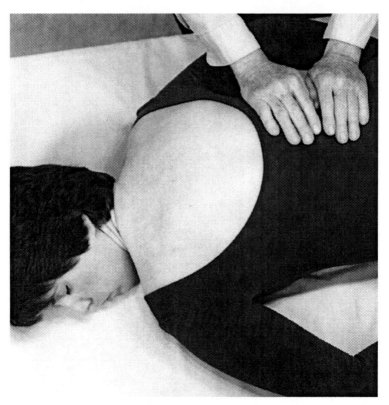

Pattern 3, Hand Position 4.

Hand Position 5:

Place your hands in a line, one in front of the other, slightly overlapping, just below the client's waist. This is good place to treat lumbar vertebra 4 (L-4) for the sciatic nerve. The sciatic nerve goes all the way down the legs. Sciatica is the name given to a painful condition that can rage all along the nerve, which can be excruciating at times. You can also add optional positions along the entire length of the sciatic nerve for treating pain. We like to treat both legs, even if only one is affected, this way, the energy flow is kept even. Your hands in position 5 will also be affecting the backside of the intestines.

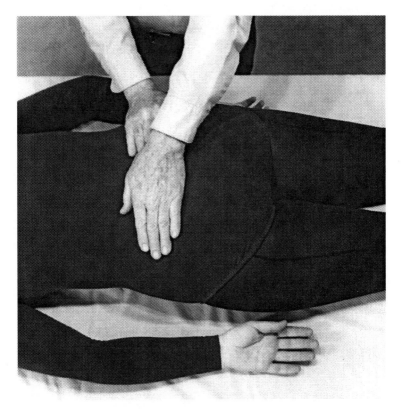

Pattern 3, Hand Position 5.

Hand Position 6:
Place your hands in a "T" position over the tailbone, which is the end of the spine, or the coccyx. This position also treats the small and large intestines, colon, bladder, anus, the male prostate gland and the female reproductive system.

The brain sends millions of messages every second to our body through the spinal nerves. Hundreds of muscles and ligaments interact with the spine. Daily tensions can create a tourniquet effect on those spinal nerves. The nerves that are supposed to be sending messages can no longer do their job. They do not reach the target.

145

Takata used to say something that John translated thus: "As in front, so in back." Very often when a client has a problem in front, they also have it in back. The spinal nerves feed the organs in the front and the back.

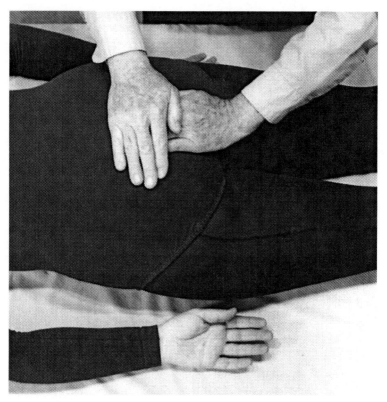

Pattern 3, Hand Position 6.

Hand Position 7:
Move your hands to the back of the knees. If the client has serious leg and knee problems, spend more time here. You can also treat the knees from the front when the client has specific knee problems.

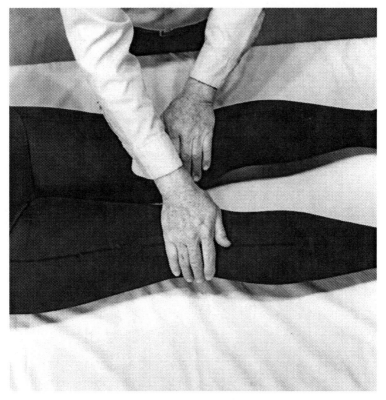

Pattern 3, Hand Position 7.

Hand Position 8:

Move your hands to the bottom of the feet. It is recommended to use a tissue, or to cover the feet with a sheet. Treat the entire plantar surface of the feet. There are reflex points on the feet that correspond to all parts of the body. Reiki stimulates these reflexes. It also helps to ground the energy, thereby improving the flow, not just for the feet and legs, but to the whole system. Finish this pattern by smoothing the energy over the top of the aura on the client's back (see step 6, below) then quietly ask her to turn over.

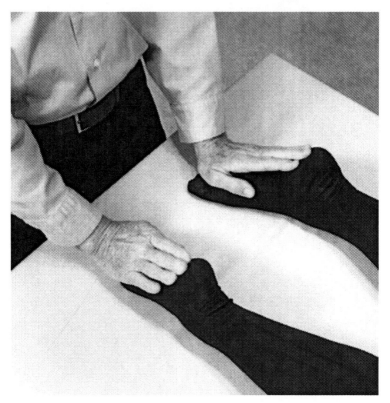

Photo 22—Pattern 3, Hand Position 8.

Step 5.—Closing Spiral

The closing spiral is the same pattern as the opening spiral of Step 3, although done in reverse (see Illustration 1 in this chapter). The practitioner begins at the client's transpersonal point above the crown chakra and ends at the heart chakra, moving in a counter-clockwise direction. When your hand reaches the heart chakra, bring your other hand up to hover just above it. You will feel the energy in both hands and it will feel complete. The closing spiral is enormously helpful in supporting clients to hold the energy so the healing process will continue after the session is over.

Step 6.—Smooth the Energy at the End of the Session

The last gesture you should make as you finish a treatment is smoothing the energy over the top of the aura. To do this, find the edge of the aura as you did when you started the session. After you find the edge of the aura, use both hands to ride this edge from the top of the head to the bottom of the feet several times in a sweeping motion. This will restore the energy flow from head to foot, one of the major flows of energy in the aura. Try to do it evenly around the body and you will feel that the flow is even. This will help the client to be more comfortable and grounded. The direction is always from head to foot, never from feet to head for that goes against the natural energy flow of a person and weakens them. From the moment of birth, energy flows from head to foot.

After the treatment ends, you may wish to lay a light blanket over the client, invite them to rest or take their time before getting up. Hydration after Reiki is important; it is appropriate to offer them a glass of water. Allow the client a few peaceful moments to absorb the whole of the treatment.

Chapter 6
Chakras and Emotions

To round out the picture of Reiki, we present in this chapter some theories about the human energy system and our understanding of how the energy system relates to deeply ingrained emotional patterns. A specific technique for scanning and assessing the energy system is fully discussed in Chapter 5. This technique may be used reliably to assess the client's physical and emotional health. A well-trained Reiki practitioner can use these techniques to plan an appropriate course of treatment.

Only medical doctors may diagnose and prescribe. Nonetheless, Reiki practitioners can gain a wealth of information about the physical and emotional state of a client by scanning the energy field of the body and then allowing that insight to guide the treatment. John developed these understandings and procedures based on his work with Hawayo Takata, Brugh Joy, M.D., and others.

John's theory of Emotionality and the Chakras asserts that the musculature, not the chakras, hold emotions. When they are not fully expressed, emotions can get locked in the body creating a state of muscular tension which prevents energy flow through the chakras. We make use of this theory with every client we see. We teach it to all our students and we recommend it to all Reiki practitioners as an effective approach to administering Reiki.

"Chakra" is a Sanskrit word for wheel. The word has come to be generally used to name the seven powerful wheels, or vortices of energy, that are part of the energetic human body. It is generally agreed upon that the purpose of the chakras is to deliver energy to the cells and organs. Explanations and diagrams of the chakras can be found in both ancient and modern writings on yoga, particularly in the Tantric disciplines of meditation and exercise. Japanese researcher Hiroshi Motoyama, in his book *Theories of the Chakras*, explains further. The chakras, in addition to being control centers for the human energy system, work as centers of "interchange between the physical and the astral and between the astral and the causal dimensions." Dr. Motoyama considers the chakras to be such a crucial part of human energy anatomy that he writes: "Chakra awakening is a process which must be undergone if the soul is to evolve and if enlightenment is to be reached."

John's education in the chakras started not with books on Eastern philosophies, but rather with Western-trained medical doctors. During studies with Richard Moss, M.D. and with W. Brugh Joy, M. D, he learned that chakra energy can be felt and assessed.

As recounted in his book, *Joy's Way*, Joy happened onto chakra energy while examining a man in his office. On impulse, he used his hand to scan the area six inches or so above the man's liver, trying to detect any energy radiating from that organ. As his hand passed from the right side of the liver to its central portion, he encountered "something that felt like a warm cloud" in the solar plexus. Astonished, he began to systematically scan a wide area above the body of the man. He also began to scan his other patients. He found and mapped uniform energy fields, cylindrical in shape, occurring in the same locations on each person. Later, while browsing in the Eastern religious section of a bookstore, he opened a book on Tantric Yoga and saw a diagram of the major energy fields. "My God," he exclaimed, "I've discovered the chakras!" John worked with doctors Joy and Moss in the late 1970s, deepening his understanding and experience.

After studying the subject for many years, we have come to believe that life energy pours into our bodies through these chakras, which appear to be centers for energy accumulation. They supply a link between our physical and non-physical bodies. We imagine the chakras as cylindrical, perhaps one-and-one-half inches in diameter, entering the body to supply the nearby meridians, glands and organs with energy.

Over many years, John developed a system that evolved both from his own perceptions of the human energy field and from his studies of the work of Wilhelm Reich. A psychiatrist and student of Sigmund Freud, Reich discovered that the muscles hold memories of past emotions or trauma and often respond by becoming chronically tense. This response, sometimes subtle, sometimes pronounced, can prevent a person from experiencing and expressing a full range of emotions. As Reich explained it, "muscles hold memory." Based on our direct experience, we agree. Muscles hold emotional memories, but harsh memories can be released to improve health.

Years ago John experienced several healing sessions with a man named Al Bauman who had studied directly with Reich. To reach the root of a particular emotion, such as sadness, Bauman had the client lie down and breathe in and out for five minutes or so. Then he would deeply massage the muscles around the throat area. The client might suddenly have a remembrance of a past sad experience and break into tears. After one or two sessions, the emotion was released from the muscles holding it, allowing the client to experience a fuller range of emotion: sadness, anger, contentment, happiness, the qualities that make daily life rich and meaningful. John discovered that Reiki can often help achieve the same results.

"When I encountered Dr. Reich's system," said John, "I understood what had happened during my childhood when I feared my father's tickling. The muscles around my solar plexus chakra had locked down on the fear of my father and future tickling. As a young child, I feared that the powerful, seemingly uncontrollable feelings aroused by tickling would lead to something terrible, death perhaps. I locked down so hard on the muscles around my solar plexus chakra that I cut off the energy flow. The band of glands and organs, supplied with energy by that chakra, became weak and vulnerable to problems."

John and Lourdes regularly give private sessions to individuals with physical problems. John says, "during the counseling session before the actual Reiki session (Chapter 5), we routinely ask the client about the physical problem, ask when the problem first surfaced, and then, the key question: what was going on at that time. In a large percentage of responses, the client tells us that he or she had been experiencing an emotional trauma either during or just before the physical problem surfaced. Recognizing the connection between the two events, the client is more easily able to work on the physical difficulty."

The significance of events is colored by our temperament and life experiences. What might deeply affect one person could be a minor nuisance to another.

Once John was giving a Reiki treatment to an economist. She had undergone a mastectomy ten years earlier. They talked about this traumatic event and the possible underlying emotional cause of her illness. This gave her an insight into her problem. Six months prior to the diagnosis of her cancer, the United States government had embarked on a fiscal policy which she was certain was going to ruin the nation. She became profoundly upset and, upon reflection, she saw that her cancer was her response to this situation.

Emotional Set-Points

"Emotional set-point" is a phrase coined by John. We use it to describe the long-term, overall emotional tone of a person. From infancy through early childhood, we humans develop emotional set-points based on experiences with siblings, parents, grandparents, caregivers, neighbors and close friends. These experiences, if profound, and especially if repeated, give rise to emotions such as happiness, fear, joy, doubt, anger, love, self-trust or self-doubt. When one of these conditions crystallizes within a person, it can be considered an emotional set-point.

Once established, these points are usually with us for the rest of our life. Like a sine curve, set-points keep popping up as we encounter words, smells, sights or other sensations that remind us subconsciously of key childhood situations and experiences.

If a set-point is an uncomfortable one, like fear, doubt, or anger, it may well get stronger and stronger until it starts communicating itself to the body. Statistically, angry people have more heart attacks than others and sad people tend to get more diseases than happy people.

Uncomfortable emotions are held in the muscles. For example, emotions relating to fear and anxiety become lodged in the muscles of the solar plexus area. The muscles then tighten up creating a tourniquet effect on the chakra's energy flow. The chakra is prevented from delivering adequate energy to the glands and organs.

If a chakra is low, or weak in comparison to the other chakras, the basis of the weakness is likely an emotional set-point which causes certain muscles to lock down. The surrounding glands, organs and other body systems receive less life force, thus becoming vulnerable to physical problems. Often Western medicine deals with symptoms, trying to ease them one way or another, without looking for the cause. The emotional set-point of a person can serve as a window, giving us a clearer view of the root causes of illnesses and allowing us to offer direct and appropriate treatment.

A Survey of the Chakras

A body worker named Rachel Claire first outlined to John the relationships between chakras, the muscles around them and emotional set-points. As John worked with these relationships, he expanded them into the system he now uses. Following is a general outline of the chakra system:

The root chakra is at the bottom of the torso, in the perineum, between the anus and genitals. It is related to an individual's self-image, an aspect subject to many double messages during early childhood. A weak root chakra can suggest that growing up, the child felt overwhelmed and hid feelings of inadequacy. He or she is unsure of his interactions with others, fearful of a hierarchy and sometimes contemptuous of those below. For example, from the shame-inducing statements children hear around toilet training or from a lack of feelings about safety and security, a child can develop a poor self-image.

A strong root chakra suggests a good self-image and basic self-confidence. These are people who enjoy life, get along with the boss and genuinely like colleagues, social events, clubs and family. People with strong root chakras understand intuitively that these realms of social activity are opportunities for learning about and helping the self. They are not afraid to admit they are not perfect and welcome opportunities to improve.

The glands and organs supplied with energy by the root

155

chakra are as follows: the penis, testicles, prostate gland, vagina, partially the colon and the legs.

The lower abdominal chakra is an inch or so below the navel. It is related to sensuality and the senses: touch, sight, hearing, smell, taste and the "sixth sense," intuition. This is where the so-called "gut feelings" originate.

When the lower abdominal chakra is weak, a person can be inhibited from utilizing his or her senses to the fullest. Patterns of behavior learned in early childhood often cause this. For example, a little boy scratches his genitals. His parents react: "Don't touch that!" So he stops touching and perhaps becomes inhibited around touch. Many children are able to see energy in various forms but are told they are imagining things and begin to mistrust their intuitive sight. Limits to sensuality can obstruct the ability to enjoy the senses, the capacity, for example, to be moved by music or to fully experience the taste of a ripe peach or the scent of a rose.

If the lower abdominal chakra is strong, the senses and the brain communicate clearly. Those strong in this area are more mindful of the scent, taste, sight, sound and touch of the world around them including sexuality, which is part of the sensual experience but not the only one. Glands and organs within the area of the lower abdominal chakra are the small intestines, partially the colon, the bladder and partially the prostate gland. An evolving consensus claims that the ovaries and the uterus get their signals from the lower abdominal chakra.

The solar plexus chakra is just below the tip of the sternum, at the center of the "V" between the ribs. When the solar plexus chakra is weak, the practitioner can be certain that from infancy and early childhood the client has had an emotional set-point around fear of the future. This fear may well be directing the client's life.

If the chakra is strong, you can suspect that this person probably thinks about the future in a positive way. He trusts in himself and his ability to handle each moment as it comes along. The band of glands and organs around the solar plexus include the stomach, spleen, pancreas, liver, gall bladder, kidneys and adrenal glands. These glands and organs are vulnerable when the solar plexus chakra is low.

The heart chakra is located between the breasts. When a Reiki practitioner notices weakness in the client's heart chakra, this suggests a pattern of anger existing from early childhood.

In the 1950s, two cardiologists, Meyer Friedman, M.D. and Ray H. Rosenman, M.D. noticed an emotional component in their work with heart patients. From their study of the phenomena, they wrote a groundbreaking book, "_Type-A Behavior and Your Heart._" This well-regarded thesis has been statistically examined many times. In brief, it states that stress associated with meeting business and professional deadlines, coupled with excessive competitive drive, might be the chief causal factor for heart attacks. Their first research effort involved a study of the normal blood cholesterol and blood-clotting rate of 40 accountants. Both rates rose alarmingly as tax-filing deadlines approached and then returned to normal levels after the deadlines had passed. From this information, large-scale studies of behaviors and patterns labeled Type A were generated.

The Type A personality is characterized by an inferiority complex twisted into a compulsion to be "the boss" in everything. Type A needs to succeed over everyone else. If the game is golf, he needs to have the lowest score. In tennis, he expects to beat the opponent every time. The resultant body armoring reduces the flow of life force to and from the heart chakra. The deprivation of this energy renders the heart and lungs vulnerable to physical problems. The client, when asked about the physical body, will usually mention heart problems or asthma.

If the heart chakra is strong, the practitioner may suspect

157

an absence of hostility, aggression, anger and likely a pattern of love. The person probably has a compassionate personality, for the self as well as others. The heart and lungs get their signals from the heart chakra. *The throat chakra* is just below the Adam's apple. If the throat chakra is weak, the practitioner may suspect this person has an emotional set-point of sadness that has run his life since early childhood. It can indicate a separation trauma within the family at an early age. This could be a single disturbing separation, like the breakup of the parents' marriage, or something small but often repeated, such as a mother heading off to work and neglecting to reassure the child that she will return. Muscles around the throat are perpetually tightened, clamped onto the memory of loneliness or sadness. The life force flowing into that area is reduced.

People with weak throat chakras seem to be more susceptible to disease in general. We have scanned many people with cancer. With the exception of two or three people, all have had a weak throat chakra. Lourdes has also scanned many people with HIV-Aids. She has noted a weak throat chakra in all of these people. This attitude of hopelessness and helplessness leads to a drop in the functioning of the immune system, which renders the self vulnerable to bacteria and viruses.

A strong throat chakra indicates a happy person, one who enjoys life and companionship but is able to be alone and not feel lonely. People with strong throat chakras are often found in occupations in which they work by themselves. Such individuals are likely to breeze through hours and hours alone, a desolation to someone with a weak throat chakra. Painters, sculptors, writers, computer programmers generally have strong throat chakras.

Glands and organs within the region of the throat chakra include the esophagus, trachea, larynx, thyroid and parathyroid glands. The thymus gland gets its signals from the throat chakra. This gland is part of the immune system and is responsible for the maturation of T cells.

The brow chakra is found in the center of the forehead, just above the eyebrows. Scanning a strong brow chakra is a rare occurrence. Individuals having a strong brow chakra tend to be involved in self-awareness and self-development activities. Meditators for the most part, they seem to be able to look both backward and forward in time and space better than most of us. They are characteristically intuitive.

Some chakra systems link the brow chakra to the pituitary gland and the crown chakra to the pineal gland, although John has not found such connections when he scans.

The crown chakra is located at the top of the head. Whenever we scan a strong crown chakra, and that is quite seldom, we know the person is deeply involved in spiritual development, one who asks for help from other dimensions: the guardian angel, the Christ Consciousness or the Higher Self.

Only about ten percent of the population will have a strong brow chakra, and those who do seem to be highly involved in personal development. Less than one percent of the population appears to have strong crown chakras and they tend to be on spiritual paths.

Throughout history, sensitive people have observed the radiant glow about the head and sometimes the whole body of particularly devout individuals. Artists have often painted it as a halo encircling the heads of great spiritual personages such as Christ and Buddha. The halo indicates a strong and awakened crown chakra.

The knees and feet are the sites of sub-chakras, smaller energy wheels. Observing the differences in strength of the left and right in a client can help the practitioner to assess the balance of yin and yang. Balance is the ideal state. Therefore, people who have the vitality of right and left side equally distributed are generally balanced in their thoughts and actions.

The left knee and foot represent the yin aspect. This aspect is equated with the feminine, intuitive, emotional, receptive nature and the right hemisphere of the brain. The right knee and foot represent the yang aspect. This aspect represents the masculine, mathematical, factual, projective, executive aspect, and the left hemisphere of the brain.

By comparing the yin and yang aspect, a Reiki practitioner can obtain insight on how the person functions within their world. When the chakras of the left knee and foot are stronger than the right, the feminine aspect predominates. This suggests someone suited to work which emphasizes the totality of situations: painting, sculpting, counseling, and so forth. If the yang aspect is stronger, this suggests a person suited to a job where the focus is on getting things done, one who pushes forward regardless of obstacles, perhaps a management or middle-management type. Comparing the chakras of the knees and feet can provide a good indication of the way the person deals with life.

In our Reiki classes, John often tells a bit about himself to illustrate this point. "My left knee and foot are stronger than my right knee and foot. I tend to get into situations where I need to be intuitive and develop information on a given subject so I can present it. Conversely, my right knee and foot, my yang aspect, my executive nature is weaker. I am slow to get things done. I am very good at processing how they should get done, but doing them is something else again."

When people have jobs that are incompatible with their basic yin-yang orientation, they often develop physical problems emerging from the side they are not emphasizing.

The Theoretical Basis for Scanning the Human Energy System

Just as it has a complex physical anatomy, the human body has a complex energy anatomy. This is something that has been known and worked with for thousands of years in the Orient, but only recently in the West.

Materialism begins with an assumption that matter alone is real; hence everything that exists is either matter or entirely dependent upon matter. But this view leaves out at least half the picture. The world in general, and human beings in particular, are also made up of forces, or energy. Reiki is a healing modality keyed to energy of the human body. Through skillful means, the practitioner links the client and the client's energy body to a vast, infinite source of a particularly beneficial band of energy frequencies. This band of energy is the basic vitalizing force at large in the universe. When a person has an ample supply of it in proper balance, they have radiant health. When the energy is depleted, they are depleted and, hence, vulnerable to illness.

Today there is an extensive literature on the human energy anatomy. We make no effort to present a comprehensive review of that literature in this book, for such an effort has been, and is being, done well by others. We offer a few key points and a list of recommended reading for readers who wish to learn more.

We affirm the reality of a human energy anatomy, a reality not only discernable via the hands of trained and experienced Reiki practitioners, but also by scientific means.

Various books from both the Orient and the West show artistic representations of the human energy system. Some designate a color for each part of the system, or a symbol, a musical note, or some other device. Some books show specific aspects of the human energy system located in one place, while other books show those aspects elsewhere. Yet other books omit some aspects altogether. This confusion will sort

161

itself out in time as our spiritual and scientific capabilities mature, for the human energy system is quite real and quite essential. At a minimum, it provides additional, different, and essential energy beyond what we receive from food, water, and air.

In the West, Harold Saxon Burr, a neuro-anatomist at Yale University School of Medicine for 43 years, uncovered and documented the existence of electromagnetic fields around living things. He conducted numerous experiments on plants, animals, and humans in order to map these life-energy fields, "L-fields," as he called them, auras as they are popularly known.

At one point Burr became interested in tracking the embryonic development of salamanders. He discovered in the embryos, an electrical axis already shaped in the form of the healthy adult animal, aligning the tail and the head. The adult energy form existed, and could be measured, while the physical salamander was still an embryo. Burr theorized that electromagnetic fields around living things serve as a matrix, or mold, to guide the future shape and arrangement of those organisms.

Burr was also successful in predicting future pathology where no clinical signs were yet detectable via standard diagnostic methods. He did this by measuring abnormal voltage patterns in the energy field. He used the analogy of a jelly mold that has a dent or a bulge, which produces dents or bulges in the jelly itself. Burr found that the electrical patterns of disease first exist in the electromagnetic field or aura before they manifest in the physical body.

Burr's finding may help us to understand how a trained Reiki practitioner can scan the body of a client with his or her hand, and actually feel not only the quantity, but also the quality of the energy.

The basic idea of an energy field around the human body was developed further by scientist Rupert Sheldrake in his theories of morphogenesis, as outlined in his landmark books: *A New Science of Life: The Hypothesis of Morphic Resonance* and *The Presence of The Past*. One of Sheldrake's important contributions was to formulate fairly loose ideas about energy fields into a testable theory. Current research into morphogenetic fields is establishing a common language, allowing energy healers and scientists to discuss and explore these realms together.

In summary, the human energy system, though not visible to the human eye for most people, is a real and essential aspect of our overall anatomy. Assessing the energy field can provide a wealth of useful information.

Within the overall energy anatomy, three major components merit attention from Reiki practitioners. These components are: the aura, or electro-magnetic field around the body; the nadis and meridians, channels or pathways along which energy flows; and the chakras, wheels or vortices of energy which transfers energy from the outside of the body to the inside.

Aura—According to Barbara Brennan's book *The Human Energy Field*, the word "aura" means "atmosphere" or "light," and is an appropriate enough term, given the nature of this phenomenon. It is usually defined as a sort of multi-dimensional energy field.." The aura can be considered a series of subtle energy bodies that surround and completely envelop each human body. It is a luminous field of energy, unique to each living being. Each of the subtle bodies that make up the human aura has a specific pattern and frequency, with a specific purpose. In general, the aura is a transitional energy field between the ordinary physical plane and the many and various planes of energy at large in the world. In analyzing the aura, we limit our observation to the segment closest to the body. This segment, which measures less than 36 inches from the physical body is considered the "physical aura."

163

Nadis—The nadis of yoga and the meridians of Chinese medicine are often considered to be essentially the same, for in their respective traditions they are recognized as the channels, or pathways, for the internal flow of vital energy (ki, chi, prana, etc.). One can picture the nadis as a dense and complex system of rivers, streams, and rivulets. Instead of carrying water or nerve impulses, the nadis carry energy. In the physical body the nadis are represented by the cardiovascular, lymphatic, and nervous systems. The nadis and the chakras are closely interrelated. The precise number of nadis in an average human being has not yet been established, but there are many. Some ancient teachings specify a total of 72,000; others say there are as many as 340,000.

Chakra—Covered previously in this chapter.

As related in Chapter 1, John's childhood fear of tickling led to adult anxiety and severe stomach problems, reflected in a low solar plexus chakra, prior to his learning Reiki. "Fear in the face of a real and present danger is a legitimate emotion," says John. "One marshals the body to deal with life-threatening situations, shifting blood supply to the arms and legs, increasing and speeding the breath and sharpening the senses to provide the best possible reaction to the fire, storm, accident, or whatever emergency has occurred. But to fear the future and to marshal the body's extraordinary capacities in defense of it, is fruitless, draining and opposes good health."

Those who drive may remember a time when another car came recklessly speeding by, through a stop sign or from the side. Such an immediate threat may have resulted in a flash of feeling in the pit of the stomach when the muscles clamped down, preparing to respond. In an instance such as this, it is fear of the present reality that causes the reactions.

Fear of the future works similarly in the body. When muscles clamp down in the pit of the stomach, they constrict the flow of life force into the solar plexus chakra. If this happens regularly, as is typically the case with people who are anxious about the future, then the band of glands and organs are deprived of the life force. They become weak and vulnerable.

In general, Reiki practitioners need to pay attention to the information received through all of their senses. Notice what your hands feel, of course. But also notice information from the other senses. When you experience an unusual sensation, such as a pain in a certain area of the stomach or a sudden smell of fear or distress, or some peculiar sort of signal that speaks to the moment, take note. The practitioner needs to ask, "How does my experience relate to my work with this client?" When you get an unusual sensation, keep it in mind. It may be a key part of the health puzzle for the client. Further, the day may come when you get another experience of that same sensation. If so you may also discern a relationship between those sensations and the health issues presented by the client. Such insight may prove to be profoundly helpful in getting to the root cause of a health problem. As Hawayo Takata said repeatedly, "Reiki is cause and effect. Find the cause and remove it and you will get rid of the effects."

566-GRAY

Chapter 7
Emergencies and
Operations

Since the beginnings of history human beings have suffered injuries requiring emergency treatment. The nature of treatment has evolved admirably through the ages and modern emergency medical interventions are rightly held in high regard. But as everyone who has ever suffered a severe injury recognizes, we can still advance. We can find new and better ways to reduce pain and speed the recovery process.

Reiki practitioners have the ability to be of crucial service in emergencies. Our experience and observations have shown us that, after an injury of any kind such as a cut, a bruise, a burn, a fracture, there is about a five-to ten-minute window before the cells disorganize. This is the place for a highly effective intervention with Reiki. The cells of the body will tend to "remember" how they were before the accident. With the support of a strong flow of healing Reiki energy, the cells affected by the injury will try to revert to their original healthy form and condition. Such emergency treatment can have an important influence on minimizing pain, swelling, disfigurement, and other consequences. Reiki can also shorten the overall time of recovery.

John came to this realization early in his Reiki career. It has been borne out by our ongoing study and experience. "When I was attuned to First Degree Reiki," John recalls, "at first I didn't feel any energy flowing through me. Takata talked about how when you practiced Reiki you would feel the energy flowing, but I didn't feel a thing. About two or three weeks later, I accidentally slammed the car door on the hand of my former wife, Beth. The pain and shock were so great that she fainted. I opened the door to free her hand, got in the car beside her and immediately held her hand to give Reiki. I just kept holding her hand, and eventually she relaxed and the pain diminished. Finally after about an hour the pain subsided. It turned out that the treatment was highly successful, even though I didn't feel anything while it was happening. There was no black-and-blue on her hand, and she had perfect flexion of her knuckles. Except for a small black spot on a fingernail, you wouldn't know that anything had happened.

"This emergency made a huge impression on me. It was a real turning point in my recognizing the value of the training I had received. I can remember thinking, 'Wow, this stuff works! And very successfully.' If Beth hadn't received Reiki right then, immediately, her hand would have been in terrible pain. She wouldn't have been able to move her knuckles. They would have been black and blue. She would have had a problem with that hand for weeks. Because of the immediate application of Reiki, she could move her knuckles perfectly well, resulting in a complete elimination of the trauma, and a restoration of her hand to full health."

This fundamental teaching about Reiki in emergencies is illustrated by a portion of the story of Mikao Usui on Mount Kurayama. When Usui, feeling elated, was rushing down the mountain after his 21-day fast he smashed into a large rock with his foot. He fell to the ground and, as is natural for everyone, reached down to hold his foot where it had been injured. A toenail was half off, he was bleeding and in pain. He continued to hold the foot, particularly his traumatized toe. After many minutes he took his hand away. The toenail was back on his foot and the bleeding and pain had stopped. He had healed his own injury. So it goes from the source on down to today: in an emergency, treat the injury directly and immediately

We have found that in the specific case of Reiki as an emergency modality, the time for effective intervention is very short: five minutes in general, and perhaps as many as ten minutes in some cases. If you were to wait for about half an hour after an injury and then treat it with Reiki, significant improvement could occur but not to the extent possible if treated during that narrow emergency window. We have seen cuts close up and become scratches, bruising that doesn't take place, very little inflammation, no formation of scar tissue later and burns disappearing without even a pink spot, all from a response within that five-minute window.

A base of scientific research may explain to a degree why the immediate application of Reiki can be an effective emergency treatment in conjunction with standard first aid. A beginning point for this study is the work of Harold Saxon Burr, Ph.D., at Yale Medical School, and of James W. Grau, Ph.D. a professor of neuroscience at Texas A&M University. As mentioned earlier, Burr studied the "L field," or human life-energy field, establishing that the energy field precedes, and serves as a kind of mold or form, for the physical cells and tissue. A healthy energy field corresponds with a healthy physical body. We believe that Reiki, rapidly applied, helps prevent distortion of the life-energy field (aura) from trauma and thereby helps prevent distortion of the injured tissue. In more recent times Dr. Grau found that, based on his research, the more quickly you properly attend to an injury and ease the pain, the more quickly you will heal and the less pain you will have. He observed that pain causes long-term changes in the spinal cord and the nerves leading to it. Thus, the less your pain systems become engaged; the less likely they are to be altered long-term by a burn or any other trauma.

Our Emergencies

In May of 1996 Lourdes had an accident while she was still living in her townhouse in Annandale, Virginia. "I was getting ready to sell the house so I could move up to New Hampshire and marry John," she explains. "It was the end of the day, I was tired and in a bit of a rush. I got sloppy. I was working outdoors with a knife and accidentally cut deep into my finger. John was with me with a garden hose nearby, so we hosed the finger off right away. We both used Reiki, got it flowing and held the cut together, applying direct pressure to the wound.

We didn't know it at the time, but what Dr. Hayashi recommended in his manual (see Appendix A) was that for cuts, you should actually squeeze the cut closed and apply Reiki, although you would not apply pressure with a regular Reiki treatment. We worked along with direct pressure and Reiki and within half an hour the cut had completely closed. I would probably have needed a minimum of five or six stitches, but because of quick and proper treatment, the cut completely closed, leaving just a scratch. We put a band-aid over it and released the shock from my adrenal glands. That was that.

Another time, John relates, came late in the summer of 1997. John was working at his computer when he noticed a problem. "As I turned from the computer toward the desk, my hand wouldn't move. I thought 'God, that's strange. Something is really wrong.' I got to my feet and was able to walk to the bed and lie down. At that moment Lourdes came in. She had been out in the garden cleaning up leaves with the leaf blower, but her intuition prompted her to come in the house. She sensed something was wrong and asked, 'can I help you?' All I could croak out was, 'ohh-ggahhh.' I couldn't speak. I'd had a stroke."

Lourdes asked John if he wanted to go to the hospital, but he refused. John was adamant and signaled: "No, do Reiki."

"I opened up the massage table," Lourdes recalls, "and got him onto it. I immediately started doing Reiki on his carotid artery (on the sides of the neck) and his head. I alternated between the carotid artery and the head." Her decision arose from Lourdes' knowledge of anatomy and the basic facts of a stroke. She knew that strokes are often caused by plaque build-up in the carotid artery. The carotid artery supplies blood to the brain. Because of plaque buildup, the blood flow to the brain can be impinged, or cut off, and that is what had happened to John.

Lourdes worked on John's carotid artery to free up the flow of blood to the brain. She also worked on the top of the head, the area where the motor muscle neurons are located, so that whatever was being traumatized there and was being denied blood and oxygen could begin working again. This also helped prevent the death of brain cells, something that often happens when stroke occurs. After a stroke, when brain cells die, the person may be left with permanent damage, such as a weakened arm and hand, slurred speech, or loss of motor control for facial muscles. If you can get to the stroke victim quickly, within the Reiki window of opportunity, then you can often prevent these occurrences.

Lourdes treated John for close to four hours. She stayed at the table and worked calmly and patiently, alternating between the two positions. The next day John went to the Marino Center, a physician-based clinic in Cambridge, Massachusetts. The doctors looked at him with astonishment. His slurred speech had gone by then, his memory was fine, and his hands and arms were normal, as though nothing had happened. John was completely fine and healthy.

"What was miraculous," John observes, "was that I had absolutely no permanent effects from the stroke. If Lourdes had not gotten to me within that five-minute window, it's likely that I would now be without movement in one of my arms, my memory might have been impaired, and I might not be able to speak."

This emergency called upon Lourdes to summon the will and the patience to stay at John's side for a four-hour treatment. "In an emergency, you rise to the occasion," Lourdes observes. "You do what you have to do. John chose not to go to the hospital and I knew that his best chance was Reiki."

This approach to the serious emergency of a stroke is not for everybody. This was John's decision. When his stroke occurred, we were out in the country, a good distance from medical aid. He chose this out of his own intuition and free will. It turned out to be the right action for him in that situation. We do not advocate anyone to hold back from contacting emergency responders and hospitals. If a medical emergency occurs, such as a stroke, we recommend that you immediately call for competent, professional medical help and apply Reiki while you are waiting for that help to arrive. Reiki is not a substitute for professional emergency response, but rather a supplement to it.

You will know how long to treat by feeling the flow of the energy. If Reiki is still flowing strongly to the affected area, stay with it. When the energy flow relaxes, which could be a while depending upon the severity of the injury, you can stop giving Reiki to it. In the case of Lourdes' laceration, it took about half an hour. With John's stroke, which was much more serious, it took about four hours.

Releasing Shock from the Adrenals

After treating any trauma or emergency, finish the treatment by releasing the shock from the adrenal glands. The reason is an important one. The adrenal glands begin to secrete adrenaline into the blood during an emergency to protect us and give our bodies extra energy to respond to it. We go into a survival mode that happens automatically when we get into a stressful situation like an accident.

Adrenaline signals the liver to release sugar into the blood stream. It accelerates the heartbeat and stops digestion. All of this is necessary and good so that we can survive the emergency, but it is not the body's normal state. We need to return the body to normal by releasing the shock from the adrenal glands when the emergency is over, otherwise a level of stress remains in the body.

In her teachings Hawayo Takata emphasized that the healing is not complete until the adrenal glands are released. She used to say, "Release the shock from the adrenal glands. There will not be complete healing after an injury if you don't release the shock from the adrenals."

To release shock, place your hands directly over the adrenals and administer Reiki until you feel the flow of energy diminish. The adrenals are located just above the kidneys in the lower back. If it is possible for the person to turn over onto his or her stomach, the correct hand placement is Pattern 3, Hand Positions 3 and 4 (see Chapter 5). If it is not possible for the person to turn over, you can access the adrenals energetically through the body with the first two positions of Pattern 1. In either case, administer Reiki until you feel the drop-off in energy.

General Guidelines for Emergencies

We recommend that all Reiki practitioners take a course in first aid and CPR (cardio-pulmonary resuscitation) from the American Red Cross. The Red Cross instructs people to first call "911," or other local emergency response phone numbers if "911" is not available in the area.

Apply Reiki directly to the injured area after or during first-aid treatment, or while waiting for emergency personnel. Remember that in an emergency, as in all cases, you can treat yourself as well as others.

Use common sense in responding to the brief "emergency window" of five to ten minutes. Once a Reiki practitioner burned her finger. She held her burned finger under cool water from the sink for a while, which is a standard first-aid response. Next she put on some ointment and bandaged the wound. Finally she was ready to sit down and apply Reiki. But by then, well over ten minutes had elapsed. The result was a burn that remained sore and painful for several weeks. She could have been applying Reiki during the emergency window while she immersed her finger in cold water and spared herself a lot of discomfort later.

Stay with the Reiki treatment until the flow of energy subsides. How long will this be? That will depend on the person and the severity of the injury. The only rule is to treat the affected site for as long as is necessary. If the injury is a broken bone or similar trauma, common sense says that Reiki is not going to repair the broken bone in some magical way. It will need to be set by a medical doctor. However, application of Reiki around the bone can help reduce or eliminate the swelling and pain around the break. When the person does have the broken bone set, the doctor will be able to slide the bones together more easily, rather than having to push the swelling aside, which can be difficult and painful.

Keep in mind that you do not need to touch the wound and risk possible infection from your hands. You can treat by holding your hands an inch or two above the injured area.

Be sure to release the adrenal glands whether you are able to give a full Reiki treatment or not. As described earlier, this is a key. If an accident has occurred and the person has an injured back, you should not move them. Wait until trained emergency personnel respond.

Operations

Surgery is akin to an accident or emergency in the sense that it has caused a trauma to the body. Although most surgeries are local and specific, the whole body is involved in receiving and processing the trauma. We suggest a full Reiki treatment for surgery candidates, both before and after the surgery, again giving careful attention to releasing the shock of the operation by treating the adrenal glands. Such a regimen will help the patient to recover more rapidly from the trauma of the operation.

If you are the next of kin, or are for any reason allowed into the intensive care room immediately following the operation, administer Reiki to the patient directly over the surgery, being sure that your hands are sanitary. If it is not possible to touch, keep your hands about one to three inches above the patient's body. You will feel the Reiki flow from your hands. It will enter the patient's life energy field and supply healthy ki energy. You may first wish to explain what you are doing to the attending doctors and nurses, who might otherwise be justifiably curious.

Try to be available to the patient at crucial times, which include immediate pre-operation and post-operation. Many hospitals now offer this option to patients. Through the staff they can schedule a treatment by hospital-approved Reiki practitioners for just before the operation and directly after. Administrators and clinicians at many hospitals around the nation have observed an improvement in patients undergoing surgery who are treated with Reiki, which is why they have instituted these programs.

As soon as the surgery is over, start giving Reiki so that

the surgical incision can be healed as quickly as possible, being sure to release the adrenals. Reiki can make a major difference in the recovery time from surgery.

If you are a Second Degree Reiki channel, you can use the absentee Reiki technique to administer Reiki to the person undergoing surgery at the very time they are actually being operated on, whether you are at home, in the hospital waiting room or chapel, or even sitting on a park bench.

Chapter 8
Reiki Mastership

Takata suffered a heart attack while in Honolulu in 1975. She was about 74 years old at the time. She realized when it happened that she was the only person in the West who was able to teach Reiki. She also knew that if she didn't create other instructors, the system would languish because, at that time, Reiki practitioners in Japan were very protective of their system. It was likely that none of them could or would ever bring Reiki to the West.

When John studied with Takata, he made over 20 audiotapes of her lectures and classes. On one of the tapes she discusses traveling to Japan in order to teach her approach to Reiki. While there, she met some Japanese citizens who were actively practicing and preserving Reiki as they understood it in Japan. Takata regarded their approach as entirely valid, but inappropriate for the West. It was highly complex, required years of training and was closely intertwined with religious practices. She felt these factors would deter students in the West and hobble the spread of Reiki through the world at a time when, in her view, it was urgently needed.

Because of this, Takata understood that she would have

to create masters in the West who could reach out to new students and adapt Reiki to a completely different culture. When it came time for her to pass on the tradition, Takata carefully selected students whom she perceived to be ripe to enter mastership training and inherit the responsibility of preserving and sowing the seeds of Reiki.

"After her heart attack," John recalls, "she asked me and two other people if we would like to become Reiki Masters. I said yes. I knew that when she died there would be no one to train and attune more practitioners. Reiki would be lost again and we would need another Mikao Usui, someone capable of that high level of sacrifice and perseverance, to recover the tradition. This is why I decided to accept Takata's invitation to become a Reiki Master."

In 1976 Takata conveyed to John the information and training necessary to become a Reiki Master. In September of that year he taught his first class, assisted by Takata. Later, at Trinity Metaphysical Center in Redwood City, California she formally acknowledged John's status as the third Reiki Master in the West and the first in California. "There were maybe 100 or 150 people at the center one Sunday night in October," John recalls. "Takata announced to everybody that I had become a Reiki Master. I came to the podium. Everyone stood up. I looked out and said, 'Everyone please sit down.' And those were my only words. I had no speech prepared, nor did I think of any. That was probably the best way of my telling people, 'I don't really know what I'm doing yet.'

"My inner experience at the time I was made a Master was, 'Holy Moses! How am I going to follow Takata? What in the world am I going to do?' I continued my work in the business world, practicing and teaching Reiki evenings and weekends until early 1979. Then I knew it was time for me to take off on my own to practice and teach full time what I had learned. Since then, one of the other two Reiki Masters passed on and the other has retired, making me the longest-practicing Reiki Master in the West."

"My first training in Reiki mastership," John continues," was learning the procedure and attunements for the First Degree class. Then Takata had to go back to Hawaii. Before she left, she said to me, 'When I come back in three months I will tell you about the Second Degree.' 'Well,' I answered, 'I've already paid the standard fee for mastership training. What will happen if you die?' Takata became flustered and angry. 'My sister in the Hawaiian Islands knows the procedure and could train you if I died,' she said. She then gave me the contact information for her sister. But three months later Takata was still alive and active. She came back to California to visit and at that time completed my training."

Takata often said she was going to retire, but she never really did. By December of 1980 when she died, Takata had trained a total of 22 Reiki Master Instructors. A year after her death, some 17 of the original Reiki Masters trained by Takata met on the island of Hawaii to mark the anniversary of her passing, and to talk about Reiki.

"We had a very special time together," John recalls. "We visited Takata's memorial, traded Reiki stories, compared attunement procedures, and planned for the future of Reiki. We could not have imagined the rapid spread of Reiki, literally everywhere around the globe. From just the 22 of us there are now hundreds of thousands, perhaps millions, of Reiki practitioners worldwide. This is wonderful, yet sometimes we regret that when we met in Hawaii we did not design a better system to accommodate this mushrooming growth because it makes the system susceptible to omissions, unplanned changes and all kinds of creative variations. In view of this, one has to wonder: when the impulse and techniques of Reiki are changed and changed again, at what point does the impulse change so radically that it is no longer Reiki, but something else?"

Bearing in mind the general nature of oral traditions and the Western inclination to speed and innovation, it is not difficult to understand why countless versions of Reiki have sprouted since the 1970s. The original 22 Masters in the West did not anticipate nor establish any kind of standards or licensing requirements for becoming a Reiki Master. As a result, one often sees, for instance, advertisements promoting combined classes for Reiki levels I, II and III (Master) in a single weekend. Some of these newly-fledged workshop participants, with no Reiki experience other than that from one weekend class, then set themselves up in business as Reiki Masters and begin to promote and teach similar workshops right away. The results of this are generations of Reiki Masters who may very well be trying to teach and preserve a tradition that they themselves have had insufficient time to experience and comprehend. While Reiki is simplicity itself at the core when accurately transmitted, it also embodies aspects that, in our view, require substantial study and experience.

We consider the spread of spiritual healing throughout the world to be a key to our survival in this new millennium and also a key to our collective spiritual growth. We applaud sincere attempts to spread Reiki as a form of healing, but we are frankly concerned about some of what is being presented in the name of Reiki.

At present there is no way for anyone to determine whether persons presenting themselves as Reiki practitioners are experienced or even properly trained. Because no specific certification or licensing procedure was ever required for Reiki Masters, much confusion exists as to qualifications. We believe the time has come to establish standards to universally identify practitioners of Reiki. We believe that those who identify themselves as Reiki Master instructors and advanced practitioners should be required, through a certification or licensing procedure, to adhere to specific teaching and practicing standards.

There are many wonderful energy healing techniques in the world. Our intention is not to disparage or discourage them, but to support dialogue and agreement on what constitutes Reiki so that when a client comes for a Reiki treatment, he or she will have a clear understanding of what they are receiving. If Reiki means anything and everything, then it means nothing. We recognize that there is much yet to be learned about bio-energy and the body's capacity to heal. Therefore, any such codification of the Reiki system must remain dynamic, willing to grow and be improved upon, based on continuing research and experience.

The Path to Mastery

If one becomes, for example, a carpenter, levels of accomplishment are attained. You begin with apprenticeship, mature as a journeyman, and eventually earn the status of Master. It is not until you really know your trade that you are recognized by your peers as a Master Carpenter and thus merit the full confidence of the public. The same holds true, in general, for electricians, bakers, plumbers, doctors, and other professions. To reach the level of mastery, practitioners must encompass the available knowledge on a subject through their study and experience.

Mastership cannot be bought. It must be earned. Nor is it something that a teacher can give or teach to a student. A teacher can only provide the tools and guidance to reach that level. With Reiki, it is practice and time invested in working with the energy that makes the difference. For this reason, along with Usui, Hayashi, and Takata, we emphasize the practice of Reiki for our advanced students and Master candidates. This allows students to cultivate an intimate and dynamic relationship with the energy. To us, the maturation of this relationship constitutes a hallmark of Reiki mastery.

Just as in the arts and the trades, a person gradually develops to become a Reiki practitioner. After a certain period of practice, depending upon the individual, a person acquires the spiritual tools and experience to be a real Reiki Master. When Reiki Mastership is just a title without the work it can go to a person's head. Reiki practitioners and instructors are human beings, no more and no less. False self-importance can only serve to separate teachers from each other and from students, instead of drawing them together in a common undertaking. We are all capable of magnificent growth and development in both our lives and healing capacities if we choose to work to attain it. A quote from Marianne Williamson expresses this thought eloquently. The quote is often wrongly attributed to South African President Nelson Mandela, who did use the quote once, with the correct attribution, in a speech at UN headquarters. The words come from Williamson's book, *A Return to Love: Reflections of the Principles of a Course in Miracles*.

> *"Our worst fear is not that we are inadequate: our deepest fear is that we are powerful beyond measure. It is our light, not our darkness, that most frightens us. We ask ourselves, 'Who am I to be brilliant, talented, beautiful, fabulous?' Actually, who are you not to be? You are a child of God, and your playing small does not serve the world. There is nothing enlightened about shrinking so that other people won't feel insecure around you. We were born to make manifest the glory of God within us. It is not just in some of us, it is in everyone, and as we let our own light shine, we unconsciously give other people permission to do the same. As we are liberated from our own fear, our presence automatically liberates others."*

The beauty and intimacy of the practice is revealed by working quietly and humbly with it, getting to know it. Just as with a flower, the petals fold back slowly, a little at a time as we give the practice our time, our attention, and our heart. In this way the capacity to heal with Reiki opens, continues to open, and to teach us. It is a lifelong process. We are always learning.

As we develop our Mastership, it will manifest itself in our lives in infinite ways, not only when we are at the table giving a session, but also in the way that we relate to other people, animals, and events. Practicing Reiki is not just working with energy, it is being partners with Spirit.

After having had the privilege and experience of attuning many thousands of Reiki students, we find that those who are seriously engaged in spiritual practices of one kind or another are easier to attune and are more open and powerful as channels than others who are not. This suggests to us a connection between the degree of spiritual practice and one's openness to Spirit.

Neither a weekend course nor or a long apprenticeship will make a person a worthy Reiki Master. Likewise, performing many Reiki sessions or doing dozens of attunements alone are also insufficient. To be a true Reiki Master in our view, one needs to strive to be of service, to understand what others are seeking, and ask, "How can I best help this person or situation?" Because ultimately, Reiki is about service and unconditional love. This is what we have learned, hand to hand, from Masters Usui, Hayashi, and Takata, and this is what we seek to pass on to you.

Appendix A:
Dr. Hayashi's Kanji
Manuscript

In 1982 John received a copy of a little book named *Leiki*, assembled by Alice Takata Furomoto. Its title, "Leiki" may be the original form of the word "Reiki," since there is no "r" sound in the Japanese language. Somewhere along the way from the Orient to the West, we believe, "Leiki" was westernized into the word "Reiki." We do not know the exact reason for the change but suppose that since there is no "r" sound in Japanese, Takata decided to change the "l" to an "r" to provide a stronger and more phonetically pleasing sound for westerners.

The *Leiki* book was a compilation of notes and photographs that belonged to Alice's mother, Hawayo Takata. The book also contained a copy of Mrs. Takata's Master Certificate signed by Dr. Chujiro Hayashi and notarized on February 21, 1938 in the City of Honolulu, Territory of Hawaii. In addition, there were some 40 pages of *kanji* (writing in Japanese characters).

John was deeply touched by this gift and understood the historical significance of the work. Therefore, he placed it in

183

his private library for safe keeping. There it sat for a long time. Some 15 years later, Lourdes was cleaning John's library and came across the little book. Lourdes possesses an insatiable curiosity for the unknown and asked John the meaning of the kanji pages. John explained that he didn't know the meaning because he never had the text translated. Lourdes quickly took the book to a translator. It turned out to be a book given to Takata by her teacher, Chujiro Hayashi, a direct student of Reiki founder Mikao Usui. The 40 pages in kanji script were identified as "an instruction manual" on how to do Leiki, a treatment guide specially established for the United States by the Hayashi Reiki Research Institute. It sets out the recommended hand placements for specific ailments and injuries.

Interestingly, the original manuscript was written with two different types of characters: a simple character that is used in Japan for people who are not that fluent in Japanese, or maybe children, and that is marked right alongside the normal, higher form of kanji. We assume that because Takata was born in Hawaii, even though she did speak and read Japanese, she wasn't as fluent as a native Japanese person; thus, we suppose that the simplified characters were put there for her benefit.

We started to explore how Takata used this manual. What fascinated Lourdes first was the manual's very subtitle. It said, "Use your fingers as an acupuncturist would use needles." Well, we wondered, what does that mean. Lourdes remembered John's story of Takata and the blind Japanese girl. After Takata gave the girl a full treatment, two things happened: the girl's blindness went away and her menstrual cycle started. Later, discussing this case with Master Acupuncturist Jayne M. Ronsicki, we learned that the liver meridian plays a major role in the reproductive system, and is the meridian which opens into the eyes. The lack of menstruation for the girl, thus, was likely a problem in the liver meridian, which simultaneously did not allow a healthy flow of energy up to her eyes.

Jayne told us that in the olden days in Japan, after a woman gave birth she wasn't permitted to do fine needlework, or anything that required strain on the eyes, because the woman's uterus had to heal and be re-energized. Apparently it was widely understood that activities that strain the eyes would influence energy in the uterus. Any strain within the liver meridian will also place stress on the kidney meridian, which is already depleted due to childbirth.

One thing that arose from these and other insights, was our interest in exploring how these acupuncture points—the meridians and the Oriental model of medicine—relate to the information and hand placements specified in this manuscript. Lourdes' impression, from what she has researched so far, is that perhaps the model of medicine at that time, for Dr. Hayashi, was traditional Chinese medicine. From there he apparently devised a system of laying on of hands to address particular medical problems, just as an acupuncturist would use his or her needles. That would explain the sub-title for the manuscript: "use your fingers as an acupuncturist would use their needles."

What follows is a translation of the 40 kanji pages from the book entitled *Leiki*. The translation was done in 1998 by June Johnson. We have rearranged the subjects into alphabetical order for the English language. We offer this material not as a guide or a recommended procedure for modern practitioners, but rather for its historical value.

Leiki Instruction Manual
Learn Techniques, Secrets, Tricks

For every treatment you offer, no matter the condition or its location, be sure to do the whole head. The head comes

185

first. For headaches treat that specific area and also the whole head.

Eyes. So many illnesses and problems we do not know all, only the doctor knows, but they can be treated with Reiki: If the problem is with the eyeball, gently touch with the finger, the tear duct and end of eye and the back of head (behind eye) four times. If the problem is with only one eye, you still have to treat both eyes. Also, for eye illness treat the pancreas, liver, uterus, and ovary. The nervous system is closely connected, and you will find it far more effective to treat the system comprehensively.

Ears. Injuries inside or outside, ringing, loss of hearing. To treat place your hands on the ear canal, the hollow behind the ear lobe, the bones behind the ear (mastoid process), and behind the head (occipital bone) for the nervous system. Treat both ears at same time, and also treat the stomach, respiratory system, lymph glands lungs, kidneys, pancreas, uterus, and ovaries.

Teeth. Treat the root area of the teeth from outside of mouth, and also the shoulders on both sides.

Mouth and Lips. If the illness is in the entire mouth, treat the mouth and also intestines. If there is an infection, something is wrong with the person's intestines and digestive system, and they require treatment. To treat the intestines, place hands in the following positions: lips, esophagus, stomach, large and small intestines, and liver.

Tongue. To treat the tongue, hold the tip of tongue (grab it) with two fingers, one above and one below the root of tongue. Also treat from outside, and treat the feet just below the arch on the plantar surface. Treat both feet at the same time.

Apathy. Treat the mouth, tongue, esophagus, stomach, intestines, liver, heart, and kidneys.

Drool. Treat the mouth, root of tongue, stomach, intestines, and the entire head.

Esophagus. Too narrow, too wide, or infected. To treat place hands on the esophagus, solar plexus—chest, stomach, liver, pancreas, kidneys, blood circulation. Most cancers do not respond especially well to treatment, including cancer of the esophagus. One should not expect very good results.

Stomach. Acid in stomach, involuntary twitching, weak stomach, hernia (stomach hanging down from scar tissue in stomach) when upset (in the head) it causes pain in stomach. So it is emotional plus upsets digestion. Nervousness can cause stomach pain and make digestion difficult. To treat lay hands on stomach, liver, pancreas, intestines, kidneys and through backbone, top to bottom. For better circulation do whole treatment.

Intestines. Constipation, appendicitis, enterostenosis, intestinal obstruction, twisted intestines (diverticulitis), diarrhea, intestinal catarrh (a condition in which there is a thick flow of mucus—as in a cold). To treat lay hands on stomach, intestines, liver, pancreas, kidneys, and heart.

Liver. Over-flow with blood, congestion, oozing, withered, shriveled. jaundice, yellow skin, cirrhosis, enlarged liver, gallstones, kidney stones. To treat place hands on liver, pancreas, stomach, intestines, heart, kidneys, blood circulation. After a couple of days of treatment kidney stones break down and pass out of the body through the urine. With cancer of the liver, can't do much about it.

Pancreas. Pancreatitis, swollen pancreas (like a hernia). To treat place hands on pancreas, liver, stomach, intestines, heart, kidneys and blood circulation.

Peritoneum. Peritonitis. To treat lay hands on liver, pancreas, stomach, intestines, peritoneum, bladder, heart, kidneys and blood circulation.

Tuberculosis. Treat same way as peritonitis.

Sickness of anus. Hemorrhoids, infected, sore, inflamed, skin dry, cracked, sphincter muscle, loss of muscle tone, weakness. Treat anus, tailbone, stomach, and intestines.

Sickness of nose. Nose swollen or shrunken from infection, illness of respiratory tract. Treat nose, throat, and lungs.

Nose bleed. To treat press each side of nose (half way down just below eyes, back of head (middle of head). At the beginning of their period some women have bleeding nose; treat ovaries and uterus.

Sinus. To treat place hands on nose, upper jaw (under nose to ears), just above both eyebrows almost to middle forehead, chest, Adam's apple, kidneys, stomach, intestines, blood circulation (entire body).

Infection of the pharynx. Pharyngitis, tonsilitis. To treat lay hands on Adams' apple, tonsils, throat, kidneys, lungs, stomach, intestines and entire head.

Throat. Trachea, bronchitis. To treat lay hands on Adams' apple, bronchial tubes, lungs, stomach, intestines, heart, kidneys and entire head.

Lungs. Pneumonia, bronchial catarrh. To treat lay hands on Adams' apple, bronchial tubes, lungs, heart, liver, pancreas, stomach, intestines, kidneys, circulation.

Urology and urinary organs. Kidney ailments, blood in kidneys, anemia, pus in kidneys, heaviness and aching in kidneys possibly due to stomach hernia, childbirth, etc. Can wear some support around stomach to keep kidney immobilized. Infection: kidney stones, uremia, uremia poisoning. To treat lay hands on kidneys, liver, pancreas, heart, stomach, intestines, bladder, entire head and blood circulation.

Bladder. Infection, unable to pass urine, a slight trace of albumen in the urine, pain upon urination. To treat place hands in same position as for kidney ailments and also treat urinary tract, prostate gland and uterus.

Bed Wetting. To treat lay hands on bladder, intestines, stomach, kidneys, spine, entire head, circulation.

Nervous System. Cerebral anemia, temporary lack of blood to head (fainting), congestion of the brain, cerebral hyperanemia. To treat lay hands on head, heart.

Hysteria. To treat lay hands on uterus, ovary, stomach, intestines and liver.

Nervous prostration, debility, nervous breakdown, insomnia. To treat lay hands on stomach, intestines, liver, pancreas, kidneys, eyes, head, circulation.

Neuralgia, neuritis. Nervous systems becomes numb, nervous spasms, being seized with a cramp, due to diseased nervous system. To treat go to the damaged area first, then

189

lay hands on liver, pancreas, stomach, intestines, kidneys, head, spinal column, blood circulation. Be cautious around uterus and ovaries.

St. Vitus' Dance. To treat lay hands on liver, stomach, intestines, kidneys, spinal column, hands, feet, head, and blood circulation.

Cerebral Hemorrhage and Coronary Thrombosis. To treat lay hands on entire head, heart, kidney, stomach, intestines, liver, and spinal column. To treat numbness in other parts of the body, also put hand there.

Brain—Meningitis. Aching, hot feelings in ears, nose, face and head, infections, may be the beginning of meningitis. It must be dealt with immediately. Lung, pneumonia, TB, feeling hot, infected—could also turn into meningitis. Take the person to a Hospital Emergency Room for evaluation. To treat lay hands behind head, and the back of the neck.

Back Problems, Cerebral Spinal Meningitis. To treat lay hands on spinal column, behind head and neck, heart, stomach, intestines, liver, kidney, and bladder. The spine, head and neck are most important to treat.

Myelitis. (Spinal cord, bone marrow): To treat lay hands on spinal column, stomach, intestines, liver, bladder, kidneys, head, and circulation.

Basedow's Disease (protruding eyeballs). To treat lay hands on uterus and ovaries, stomach, intestines, liver, pancreas, heart, lymph canal, eyes, kidney, spinal column, and blood circulation.

Children's Diseases. Paralysis, palsy, numbness. To treat lay hands on spinal column, stomach, intestines, kidney, and on the site of disease where numbness is, head, and circulation.

Contagious Diseases. Dysentery, cholera, also children's cholera To treat lay hands on stomach, intestines, liver, pancreas, kidneys, heart, head, and circulation.

Typhoid Fever, Para-typhoid fever. To treat lay hands on liver, pancreas, stomach, intestines, heart, kidney, spinal column, and head.

Measles. To treat, lay hands on Adams' apple, windpipe, trachea, stomach, intestines, heart, kidneys, spinal column, and head.

Scarlet Fever. To treat lay hands on Adams' apple, chest area, kidneys, stomach, intestines, bladder, head and blood circulation.

Chicken Pox. To treat lay hands on stomach, intestines, kidneys, blood circulation, put hands on problem area and entire head.

Influenza. To treat lay hands on nose, Adams' apple, windpipe, trachea, lungs (chest area) liver, pancreas, stomach, intestines, kidneys, head and blood circulation.

Whooping Cough. To treat lay hands on nose, Adams' apple, trachea, apex of lung, stomach, intestines, kidneys and blood circulation.

Diphtheria. To treat lay hands on Adams' apple, windpipe, nose, lungs, heart, liver, stomach, intestines, kidneys, entire head and blood circulation.

Weil's Disease. To treat lay hands on liver, pancreas and spleen at the same time, stomach, intestines, bladder, kidneys, spinal column, entire head, and blood circulation.

Malaria. To treat lay hands on pancreas and spleen at the same time, liver, heart, stomach, intestines, kidneys, spinal column, entire head and blood circulation.

Tetanus. To treat lay hands on jaw bone, back of head only, Adams' apple, lungs, area of the tetanus problem, stomach, intestines, kidneys, and spinal column.

Articular Rheumatism. There are two types of Rheumatism here, joint and muscular; they are treated in the same way. First treat the problem area, then heart, chest area, liver, pancreas, stomach, intestines, kidneys, spinal column, and entire head.

Dog Bite by Rabid Dog. First treat the problem area, then, heart, liver, kidneys, stomach, intestines, spinal column, Adams' apple, entire head and blood circulation.

Sickness of Whole Body. To treat lay hands on heart, liver, pancreas, stomach, intestines, kidneys, spinal column and blood circulation. (Anemia and Scurvy are treated the same).

Diabetes. To treat lay hands on liver, pancreas, heart, stomach, intestines, bladder, kidneys, head, spinal column and blood circulation.

Obesity. To treat lay hands on liver, pancreas, heart, stomach, intestines, bladder, kidneys, entire head, spinal column and blood circulation.

Sickness of Skin: To treat lay hands on stomach, intestines, liver, kidneys, the skin problem area and blood circulation.

Scrofula. To treat lay hands on area of skin problem, stomach, intestines, liver, heart, chest, kidneys, spinal column and blood circulation.

Constant, excessive perspiration. To treat lay hands on kidneys and blood circulation.

Burns. To treat hold hands about an inch above the burn. After pain has gone, put hands on lightly.

Sword Cuts. To treat put thumb or hand on it to stop the bleeding, pinching area closed.

Fainting or Electrocution. To treat resuscitate the person first, then place hands on heart and head.

Drowning. To treat remove water from lungs, resuscitate, heart and head.

Menstruation Cramps. Treat uterus, both ovaries, and pubic bone.

Hiccups. To treat place hands just below lungs, liver, pancreas, kidneys, stomach, intestines, spinal column, and head.

Stuttering. To treat place hands on Adams' apple and head. Also, the client should practice alone singing simple songs.

Pain in Fingertips. To treat place hand on the problem area.

Vomiting. To treat place hands on stomach, apex of stomach, bottom of lungs, liver, hands on back on spinal column just behind stomach, head and kidneys.

A Thorn or Splinter In Ones' Finger. To treat press gently on the problem area with finger; after pain has gone pull out thorn or splinter.

Gonorrhea. For a female treat the urinary tract, vulva, bladder, uterus. For a male place hands lightly and carefully on testicles.

Spasms, Hysterics, Stomach Cramps. To treat place hands on stomach, on the back just behind stomach, liver, kidneys, intestines and head.

Hernia. Lightly touch the problem area and it will shrink. Also treat the stomach and intestines.

Pregnancy And Infants' Diseases

Morning Sickness. To treat lay hands on uterus, stomach, apex of stomach, intestines, kidneys, entire head and spinal column.

Fetus not Positioned Right for a Normal Delivery. To treat lay hands on uterus.

To Work on Pregnant Women. Lay hands on uterus.

To Assist Pregnant Women During Delivery. Put hands on sacrum and on back of each hip bone.

Still Birth: If you treat the fetus while still in the womb by placing your hands on the uterus, the fetus will come out that day or the next day.

Mother's Milk Drying up. To treat massage breasts. If the mother receives Reiki energy this way, milk will start immediately.

Convulsive fit. To treat lay hands on heart, head, stomach, and intestines.

Congenital Syphilis. To treat first lay hands on the area of disease, then, give natural medication to cleanse the body of poison.

Erysipelas. First treat the problem area, then stomach, intestines, liver, heart, kidneys, spinal column, and blood circulation.

-End-

Appendix B:
Chakra Meditation

W e often use the meditation below in our First Degree Reiki classes to bring students into a quiet place and to help them open their chakras. We suggest that you go through each of the meditative suggestions five or more times. Some of our students have recorded the meditation onto a cassette, which they play as they enter the meditation.

Close your eyes—Breathe slowly and evenly through your nose. In and out, breathing into your center of consciousness and out through your nose. . . . . .

Breathing evenly, perhaps no break between the in-breath and the out-breath. . . . . .

As you breathe, visualize that you are picking up petals of love from your center of consciousness and breathing them out your nose as love energy. . . . . .

Breathe in, now, and breathe out through your crown chakra. Into your center of consciousness and love energy out the crown chakra......

Breathe in, now, and breathe love energy out through your brow chakra—your third eye—Look up at your third eye through your closed eyes if you wish......

Send love energy out your throat chakra, now. Release and relax muscle memories of past sadnesses centered around the throat......

Now breathe petals of love out the heart chakra. Fill the room with petals of energy from your heart center......

Breathe out through the solar plexus chakra. Release and relax muscle memories of past fears, past anxieties centered around this chakra......

Breathe out through the lower abdominal chakra, just below the navel. Open this center with your petals of love so it can funnel in more life energy from the outside......

Now breathe through the root chakra, located between the genitals and the anus. See the root chakra opening fully, so it too can funnel in more life energy from the outside......

Breathe out through the feet. Visualize yourself standing tall, feet firmly planted on the ground, knowing who you are and what you represent. Allow energy from Mother Earth to flood up through your feet into your solar plexus, where it joins with the energy from Father Sun flooding down through your crown to create a tremendous furnace of personal power......

Now breathe the petals of love out through all chakras at the same time. . . . . .

As you prepare to conclude the meditation, count down slowly and steadily from 10 to 1. As you progress in the count you will become progressively more awake, alert, and happy—feelings that will continue through the day. When you reach the number 1 all of your five physical senses will be operating cleanly, clearly, sharply and beautifully. Wiggle your fingers and toes to stimulate circulation, and have a good stretch. . . . . .

The meditation is over.

Recommended Reading

Autobiography of a Yogi, by Swami Paramahansa Yogananda. Self-Realization Fellowship, 1946.

Beyond Biofeedback, by Elmer and Alyce Green. Dell Publishing Co., 1989.

Energy Medicine: The Scientific Basis, by James L. Oschman, Ph.D. Churchill Livingstone, 2000.

The Future of the Body: Explorations Into the Further Evolution of Human Nature, by Michael Murphy. Jeremy P. Tarcher/ Putnam, 1993.

Healing Visualizations, by Gerald Epstein, M.D. Bantam Books, 1989.

The Holographic Universe, by Michael Talbot. HarperCollins Publishers, Inc., 1992.

Joy's Way: A Map for the Transformationa l Journey, by W. Brugh Joy. J.P. Tarcher, Inc., 1979.

Mastery: The Keys to Success and Long-Term Fulfillment, by George Leonard. Plume, 1992.

Meditating With Children, by Deborah Rozman. University of the Trees Press, 1988.

Molecules of Emotion: Why You Feel The Way You Feel, by Candace B. Pert. Scribner, 1997.

Natural Alternatives to Over-the-Counter and Prescription Drugs, by Michel T. Murray. William Morrow and Company, 1994.

A New Science of Life, by Rupert Sheldrake. Times Books, 1988.

The Presence of the Past, by Rupert Sheldrake. Times Books, 1988.

Quantum Healing: Exploring the Frontiers of Mind/Body Medicine. By Deepak Chopra. Bantam, 1989.

Readings on the Scientific Basis of Bodywork, Energetic, and Movement Therapies, by James L., Oschman, Ph.D. and Nora H. Oschman. Collection, 1997 (P.O. Box 5101, Dover, NH 03821).

Reiki: The Hawayo Takata Story by Helen J. Haberly. Blue Mountain Publications, 1990.

Reiki Fire, by Frank Arjava Petter. Lotus Light Publications, 1997.

The Roots of Consciousness: The Classic Encyclopedia of Consciousness Studies, by Jeffrey Mishlove and S.P. Sirag. Marlowe & Format, Inc., 1997.

Superstrings: A Theory of Everything, by P.C.W. Davies. Cambridge University Press, 1995.

Superstrings and the Search for the Theory of Everything, by David F. Peat. Contemporary, 1988.

Theories of the Chakras: Bridge to Higher Consciousness, by Hiroshi Motoyama. Theosophical Publishing House, revised edition 1997.

The Tao of Physics: An Exploration of the Parallels Between Modern Physics and Eastern Mysticism, by Fritjof Capra. Bantam, 1991.

Type A Behavior and Your Heart, by Meyer Friedman, M.D. and Roy H. Rosenman, M.D. Fawcett Crest, 1975.

Treating Type A Behavior and Your Heart, by Meyer Friedman and Diane Ulmer. Fawcett Books, 1985.

What is 'Healing Energy'? The Scientific Basis of Energy Medicine, by James L., Oschman, Ph.D. from the Journal of Bodywork and Movement Therapies, 1996.

Wholeness and the Implicate Order, by David Bohm, Routledge, NY, 1996.

66-GRAY

Some Relevant Studies

The Effect of Non-Contact Therapeutic Touch on the Healing Rate of Full Thickness Dermal Wounds, by Daniel P. Wirth, M.S. J.D., Subtle Energies, Volume I, Number 1, 1990.

The Laying on of Hands; Implications of psychotherapy, Gentling, and the Placebo Effect, by Bernard Grad. Journal of the American Society for Psychical Research, 1967, 61(4), 286-305.

Some Biological Effects of the 'Laying on of Hands': A review of Experiments with Animals and Plants, by Dr. Bernard Grad, Journal of the American Society for Psychical Research, 1965.

Wound Healing Research Through the Ages, by Henry Brown, MD, from the book *"Wound Healing: Biochemical and Clinical Aspects,"* edited by Jennifer Mitchell, 1992, W.B. Saunders Company, Philadelphia, PA.

About the Authors

Reverend John Harvey Gray has been a Reiki Master Instructor since 1976, actively teaching and practicing Reiki longer than any other living teacher. He has taught over 750 workshops and trained more than 10,000 students. In 1974, John became one of the first three of the original 22 Reiki Master Instructors trained by Hawayo Takata, the woman who brought Reiki to the United States from Japan. He took his entire Reiki training with Mrs. Takata and continues to teach according to her time-honored tradition. John's early education took place in California and the Far East. He later graduated from Dartmouth College. After serving in World War II, his careers before Reiki included banking, computer systems development and research at Stanford Research Institute.

John's wife and business partner, Lourdes Gray, has taught over 200 Reiki workshops since becoming a Reiki Master Instructor, certified by John from Hawayo Takata in 1996. Born in Cuba, Lourdes worked in real estate and mortgage banking before becoming a full-time Reiki practitioner. Her

566-GRAY

Reiki practice includes the treatment of chronic diseases as well as emotional problems. Her classes incorporate her life-long interest in both scientific and esoteric energy theories while continuing to work within the Usui-Gray tradition. She holds a Bachelor of Science degree in Natural Health.

Both John and Lourdes are ordained ministers in the Church of the Loving Servant, a non-denominational church founded by John and devoted to spiritual healing. Together they continue to share a life of Reiki teaching, research, healing and development of the Usui-Gray Integrated Reiki System®.

Journalist Steven McFadden is also the author of *Profiles in Wisdom: Native Elders Speak About the Earth* (iUniverse.com, 2000), *Legend of the Rainbow Warriors* (2001) and *Farms of Tomorrow Revisited* (1998). In August, 2000, under the instruction of John and Lourdes, he became a Reiki Master in the Usui-Gray tradition.

Elisabeth Clark, artist, writer, ethnic dancer and world traveler has been publishing articles, stories and poems for over a decade. She became acquainted with Reiki in 1998 through her painting. She is presently training with John and Lourdes for her Reiki mastership.

The John Harvey Gray Center for Reiki Healing is located on Lake Monomonac, nestled in the foothills of New Hampshire's famed Mount Monadnock. Reiki classes, private instruction and treatments are held here, along with bi-monthly donation-based Reiki healing sessions.

The John Harvey Gray Center for Reiki Healing
P.O. Box 696, Rindge, NH 03461
www.reiki.mv.com

Printed in the United States
57781LVS00002B/75

9 781401 049607